D1433337

Run, John, Run

The Second Volume of Radio 2
Janet & John Stories

Kevin Joslin

headline

First published in 2011
by HEADLINE PUBLISHING GROUP

This edition published 2011 for Index Books Ltd

1

Cataloguing in Publication Data is available from the British Library

ISBN 978 0 7553 6185 4

Typeset in Plantin MT Schoolbook by Avon DataSet Ltd,
Bidford-on-Avon, Warwickshire

Printed and bound in Great Britain by
Clays Ltd, St Ives plc

Headline's policy is to use papers that are natural, renewable and
recyclable products and made from wood grown in sustainable forests.
The logging and manufacturing processes are expected to conform to the
environmental regulations of the country of origin.

HEADLINE PUBLISHING GROUP
An Hachette UK Company
338 Euston Road
London NW1 3BH

www.headline.co.uk
www.hachette.co.uk

Flick the pages!
See Janet chase John!

For my parents Joe and Maureen,
who always hoped that I might one day
have a 'proper job'.
Sorry about this . . .

Also to the memory of my grandfather,
George Madle, who left me his greatest
bequest – my sense of humour.

Contents

Foreword
By Sir Terry Wogan

Once more the innuendo and double-meaning that fester just below the surface of these tales of simple folk rise to affront the sensibilities of the delicately reared. Do not approach without the sal-volatile! Hats off to Kevin Joslin for his inspired if warped creativity, and to your good self for buying the stories that have contributed so much to Children in Need.

Introduction

Thank you for buying this second volume of the Radio 2 Janet and John stories. I first started writing the stories back in 2005 and had no inkling that they would become as popular as they are.

But all things must pass, and as John Marsh will not be appearing on Sir Terry's new Sunday show, this will probably be the last of the stories published. I could have never imagined that they would ever be published at all, so the commissioning of this second volume is a testament to the public's continued appetite for smutty innuendo and double entendres.

Sales of the BBC CDs of the stories continue to raise much-needed funds for BBC Children in Need, and have, to date, contributed more than £4,000,000. The CDs are still available from www.charitygoods.com and not one penny of the (very reasonable) sale price is spent on overheads, wages or administration.

Should anyone feel inclined, I can occasionally be found on both Twitter and Facebook if you look hard enough.

Acknowledgements

I would like to give special thanks to my publisher, Headline, and my literary agent, Darin Jewell. Both have continued to do wonderful work on my behalf.

I would also like to pay tribute to the scores of 'characters' in the stories. With the possible exception of Pastor Kidneys (who although fictitious, was heavily based on Canon Roger Royle) and Donatella, the hairdresser, all of those featured in the tales are real people, many of whom are my friends, and all of whom deserve some form of recognition for the lampooning they have taken over the years. However, there is only room for the most regular victims (and those that I think might hit me if they are not mentioned). So, special apologies (especially to anyone who feels that they should have been included) go to Sally Dickins, Julie Wiseman, Tina Philips, Gail Holland, Jo Plumb, Jacki Havard, Jen Terris, Lesley Brown, Jen O'Brien, Jane Edwards, Roger Spicer, Ann Myers-Brotherston (Mrs Bickerdyke), Pauline Robbins (Melanie Frontage), Helen and Norman Mackintosh, Barbara Mason, Lucy Sibley, Julie Frost, Franki Ayerst, Irene Forrest, Geraldine Coleman, Terri Reddington, Anne Dempsey, Karen Lee and my fellow (proper) writer Lyndsay Jones.

Very best tickles are reserved for Janet and John Marsh, Phil 'Nobby' Hughes, Alan Boyd, Alan Dedicoat and last but by no means least, the man I have been honoured to write for, the delightful Sir Terry Wogan.

Finally, a loud and somewhat splashy raspberry

to the unnamed company (you know who you are) who continue to make life as difficult as possible for the BBC, who have used these stories to raise much-needed funds for Children in Need.

Kevin Joslin

October 2011

John Goes to a Café

Today, John is at work.

John has a part-time job reading things out on the radio for money.

Do you like money? John does.

John spends nearly all of his money on clothes made of silk, satin and lace. John is a fop.

John is going to a café for lunch before he goes home. John likes to eat cakes, buns, sandwiches and sweets.

See John's funny round belly.

See John hop and skip along the road to the café.

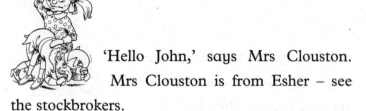 'Hello John,' says Mrs Clouston.

Mrs Clouston is from Esher – see the stockbrokers.

John says, 'You are very busy today Mrs Clouston.'

Mrs Clouston says, 'Yes, Mr Clouston is off playing golf again. It's only me and Mrs Buckingham here today and we are rushed off our feet.'

Poor Mrs Clouston.

John says, 'I have finished work for the day, would you like a hand?'

'Yes please,' says Mrs Clouston.

Kind John.

Mrs Clouston says, 'You'd better put on an apron, that silk brocade frock coat will get very dirty otherwise.'

See John spend ten minutes finding an apron that 'goes'.

See Mrs Buckingham get some mugs ready to make hot drinks.

John says, 'I like these coffee mugs. The yellow and black stripes are very pretty. They look like

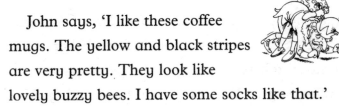

lovely buzzy bees. I have some socks like that.'

Mrs Buckingham says, 'I will pour out the coffee from this machine. I'd like you to put the whipped cream on the top for me please.'

Do you like whipped cream?

See John putting cream on top of the mugs and helping Mrs Clouston to serve the cakes.

Soon lunchtime is over, and Mrs Clouston thanks John for all his help and gives him a big mug of hot chocolate and as much gateau as he can eat.

See John wave goodbye to the ladies as he goes to catch the train home.

When John gets home, Janet is cleaning out the freezer.

Janet says, 'You're late today John.'

John says, 'Yes. I popped out to get some lunch, and saw Mrs Clouston and Mrs Buckingham. Mr

Clouston was out and they were both looking forward to getting their feet up so I took his place. Mrs Buckingham unhooked and warmed up a pair of bee-cups then held them out while I put whipped cream on them, and afterwards Mrs Clouston let me have as much of her Black Forest as I could eat at one sitting.'

Do you know how to make steam come out of your ears?

Janet does.

See Janet shut John's head in the freezer door. Hear the screams.

Poor John.

Janet and John Go to an Antiques Fair

Today, Janet and John are going to an antiques fair.

Janet likes antiques. See the credit card bills.

Janet says, 'Don't take too long getting ready John.'

'I'm nearly ready,' says John. 'I just have to put on my beauty spot.'

John is dressed in a lilac frock coat, silver and black striped waistcoat, a frilly shirt and a powdered wig. John is a dandy.

When Janet manages to pull John away from

the mirror, they drive to the antiques fair.

The antiques fair is in a very big hall. Janet says, 'Why don't you go and play with the other children while I look around? And do try not to get into trouble!'

'I won't,' says John.

See John run round and round the hall and do big slides on his knees on the polished floor. Naughty John.

When John is quite tired, he stops near a stall selling stamps. John likes stamps.

The ladies running the stall introduce themselves as Mrs Domone and Mrs Locket.

John says, 'I have some nice stamps at home in an album.'

Mrs Domone says, 'Have you been collecting for a long time?'

John says, 'Yes, ever since I was very young.'

John says, 'I have some very nice Victorian stamps in an old album. I like the pretty purple ones best.'

Mrs Locket says, 'If you have any of the purple Tannenburgs, I'd be very interested in seeing them, but you have to be so careful with them as the gum can cause discoloration if they are not mounted properly.'

Mrs Domone says, 'I have one here. It's not in very good condition – we say "touched" in the trade – but if you are interested, we could let you have one at trade price.'

Mrs Locket says, 'We also have some very nice correspondence from some of Louis the Fourteenth's court officials if you like that sort of thing.'

Do you like spending money? John doesn't. John is a skinflint.

John says, 'Thank you, I will think about it.'

He hops and skips off to find Janet.

Janet says, 'Have you been a good boy, John?'

'Yes,' says John. 'I saw Mrs Domone and Mrs Locket. Both ladies were very interested in my purple Tannenburg and showed me a slightly touched one under the counter. They said they didn't even mind a bit of gumming. Mrs Domone said that something a bit more subtle than a rough mounting would be needed to bring out the best in it. Mrs Locket said that she also had a nice selection of French letters if I was interested in that sort of thing.'

See Janet stand on John's beard and show him some really big stamps.

Poor John.

Janet and John Go to a Country Show

Today, it is a lovely sunny day and Janet and John are going to a country show.

See John put on his pink and orange tweed plus fours with yellow socks, black and pink brogues, a bright yellow sleeveless jumper and a white shirt with a purple tie. See The Open.

Janet says, 'Hurry up John, otherwise the queue for the car park will be enormous.'

See John hop and skip out to the car.

As it is a long drive, see Janet pack some spare pull-ups and John's best Dora the Explorer potty.

When Janet and John arrive at the country show, Janet parks the car in a big meadow and puts on John's reins to stop him running around near the tractors.

Can you make a noise like a tractor? John can't.

Janet says, 'I'm going to get in the queue for the hog roast, why don't you go to look at some of the livestock displays? I'll see you back here in half an hour.'

See John wave to Janet as he hops and skips gaily to the big marquees to look at all the animals.

In the first tent, John sees lots of goats. See John laugh at a goat called Snowy and how silly she looks with her long white whiskers.

In the next tent, there are lots of chickens, ducks and caged birds.

John likes birds, but they often go after his plums.

John sees Mrs Bradley.

'Hello John,' says Mrs Bradley.

John says, 'Hello Mrs Bradley.  What are all these birds here for today?'

Mrs Bradley says, 'They are in a competition to win prizes for the best of breed and best in show. I am showing some of my bantams. I breed a variety called the silkie, they are in the cage behind me. If you climb under the table you can see them up close. They are next to my Sussex pullet.'

John says, 'Thank you Mrs Bradley, they are very nice.'

See John looking at lots of the caged birds, parakeets, lovebirds and finches.

John sees Mrs Middleton.

'Hello Mrs Middleton,' says John. 'Have you put some of your chickens into the competition too?'

Mrs Middleton says, 'Not today John. I am one of the judges. I have just awarded the prizes for the best caged birds. I gave second place to Mr Bradley's zebra finches, but Mr Tow the Postman's finches were breathtaking – a dozen of the finest I've ever seen. They will win the best caged birds today. If you come back a little later, I'll be judging the chickens and I think that the old English game variety should do very well.'

'Thank you Mrs Middleton,' says John.

See John skip back to see Janet.

Janet is near the front of the queue for the hog roast. Do you like roast pork? John does.

'Hello John,' says Janet. 'Did you have a nice time?'

'Yes,' says John. 'I saw Mrs Bradley first. She was quite happy to let me duck under the table and look at her silkies and pullet. Then I saw Mrs Middleton. She was saying that she'd normally let me enjoy the game birds, but Mr Tow had left her quite breathless with his magnificent entry of twelve finches. But she said if I came back later she rather fancied an old English game.'

Can you mount a whole newsreader on a roasting spit? Janet can.

See Janet fetch a big bucket of marinade.

Poor John.

John Goes to the Corner Shop

Today, John is going to the corner shop.

Janet gives John a list of things to buy and a nice crisp ten-pound note.

Janet says, 'Don't be too long as I want a hand defrosting the chest freezer.'

See John put the money and the shopping list in his leopard-skin clutch bag and hop and skip down the road to the local shop.

See John stop by the estate agent's office and play funny games with his reflection in the shop window. See Harry Worth.

John goes into the shop and 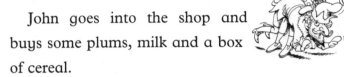 buys some plums, milk and a box of cereal.

On the way out of the shop, John sees Mrs Phizackerley-Sugden.

'Hello Mrs Phizackerley-Sugden,' says John.

John is very good at pronouncing long names.

Mrs Phizackerley-Sugden is standing by her car. John sees that the bonnet of the car is up.

John says, 'Have you got some trouble with your car?'

Mrs Phizackerley-Sugden says, 'Yes, I just noticed that the hooter on the car was not working again and I was just having a look to see if I could mend it. My husband tried to do it over the weekend, but it's still not working properly.'

John says, 'Let me see if I can fix it for you.' Kind John.

John looks at the electrical connections and gives them all a good wiggle.

John says, 'Try that.'

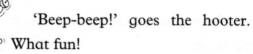

'Beep-beep!' goes the hooter. What fun!

John says, 'It was just a loose connection.'

Clever John.

Mrs Phizackerley-Sugden says, 'Oh, thank you John. My husband is getting a bit old to fix cars. Would you like me to give you some free advanced driving lessons?'

John says, 'Thank you, but I already have a licence.'

Do you have some points on your licence? John does. See Pitlochry.

Mrs Phizackerley-Sugden says, 'If you pass your advanced driving test, it will reduce the cost of your insurance.'

See John jump into the driving seat and do a racing start. John is a skinflint.

Mrs Phizackerley-Sugden and John drive around the block and do an emergency stop.

Mrs Phizackerley-Sugden has to catch some of

John's shopping to stop it falling on the floor.

'Very good,' says Mrs Phizackerley-Sugden. 'You are a very good driver John. Call me if you would like some more free lessons.'

'I will,' says John.

See John skip and caper all the way home.

When John arrives home, Janet says, 'You were gone a long time John.'

John says, 'Yes. On the way back from the shops, I saw Mrs Phizackerley-Sugden. She told me that her husband couldn't get the horn working because of his age. When she eventually told me to stop, she had to catch my plums to stop them rolling on the floor. She said I probably pulled out a bit quickly after signalling my intentions, but said that I was very good and she'd be happy to take me out any time.'

Do you know how to do an icy stare? Janet does.

See Janet push John into the freezer and shut the lid.

Poor John.

Janet and John Go to the Health-food Shop

Today, Janet and John are going to the health-food shop in the village.

Janet says, 'I'm afraid that you are eating too many crisps and sweets John, so we are going to pick up some healthy snacks to see if we can get rid of that pot belly of yours. Hurry up and get ready.'

John quickly puts on some clothes – a bombazine bolero jacket, black silk trousers with pink flowers around the waist, a purple sash and a frilly pink shirt – and in less than two hours is ready to leave.

John is a popinjay.

When they arrive in the village, Janet says, 'Here's the money for the snacks, I'm going to the bank. I'll see you outside in twenty minutes. Do try to behave.'

'I will,' says John, as he takes the money from Janet and hops and skips gaily down the road to the health-food shop.

Soon, John is outside the health-food shop and is looking in the window at all of the pills and potions.

John sees Mrs Henderson. 'Hello, Mrs Henderson,' says John.

'Hello John,' says Mrs Henderson.

What fun!

Mrs Henderson is from Ilford. See the stilettos.

'Are you looking for a cure for something?' says Mrs Henderson.

John shakes his head. 'Janet says I have to stop eating so many sweets and crisps and buy something healthy.'

Mrs Henderson says, 'Very sensible. I have to stay fit and healthy as I work with sports people.' Clever Mrs Henderson.

See John and Mrs Henderson go into the shop.

John picks up lots of packets of dried fruit, nuts and seeds and takes them to the counter to pay.

Mrs Henderson is already at the counter. See John waiting patiently.

Mrs Kendall who is serving says, 'Perhaps you'd both be interested in this? It's a new dehydrated beer supplement. It's only fifty pence a bottle.'

Do you know what dehydrated means. John's friend Alan does.

John says, 'I'm not allowed to drink beer.'

Mrs Kendall says, 'Take some for Janet then. It's not for drinking anyway, you just take one tablet a day and you get all the health benefits of a glass of beer without getting drunk.'

Do you know what 'missing the point' means?

Mrs Henderson says, 'I'll take some of those

please. I don't really like beer very much. I prefer champagne.'

Mrs Kendall gets two bottles out from under the counter and says, 'These will certainly put a flush back in your cheeks, and Janet's too.'

John pays for all the things he has bought and runs down the road to meet Janet.

'Hello Janet,' says John.

Janet says, 'Did you behave?'

'Yes,' says John. 'I went straight to the health-food shop. I saw Mrs Henderson outside. Mrs Kendall said that she had something that I ought to try under the counter for fifty pence. Mrs Henderson was first, but both of them said that fifty pence for a good healthy "beer dried" was a bargain and that you should give it a try as it would put some colour back in your cheeks too.'

See Janet put her hands around John's throat and get some colour back into his cheeks.

Do you think blue is a nice colour for cheeks?

John doesn't. Poor John.

Janet and John
Go to the Airport

Today, Janet and John are going to the airport.

John likes going to the airport.

Janet and John are not going on a plane today. John is picking up some new clothes that he has bought on the Internet, which have been sent by courier.

Do you know how to use the Internet?

John does.

John puts on his best airport clothes – a pilot's uniform with lots of gold braid, fake medals and a big cap with a shiny peak.

When they arrive at the courier's office, John hands over the paperwork to the lady at the front desk. See the lady checking the computer.

'Your parcel hasn't arrived at the offices yet,' she says.

See John blub.

The lady says, 'It's alright though as it's over at the airport offices. Mrs Frost is just about to drive over there. Would you like to go with her?'

'Yes please,' says John.

Janet says, 'I'll stay here and have a cup of coffee, but do try and behave!'

John says, 'I will.'

Mrs Frost says, 'Hello John. Hop in the van and we will soon have your parcel. Feltham isn't too far from Heathrow.'

When they arrive at the parcel office, they have to go through security to make sure they are not carrying anything naughty. John is very glad he didn't bring his catapult.

Mrs Frost says, 'It's a good job I decided to come into the office today. I'm supposed to have Mondays off.'

Mrs Frost speaks to her friend Helmut on the phone, scans John's handbag with a little machine and completes the paperwork. Soon John has his parcel.

'Thank you Mrs Frost,' says John.

When they get back to the office to meet Janet, Janet is waiting by the warehouse door. Janet says, 'Did you get your parcel John?'

'Yes,' says John. 'As soon as she sniffed my bag, Mrs Frost put in a lot of work on my part. She said it was a good job she came in today as she normally has it off. No sooner had she asked for Helmut than it was in her hands.'

Can you use one of the machines that wraps a parcel in clear plastic? Janet can.

See Janet stick a big 'Moscow Express' sticker on John and push him through the parcel hatch.

Poor John.

John Goes to the Delicatessen

Today, Janet and John are going into Uckfield.

Do you know where Uckfield is?

John puts on his best shopping clothes – a zebra-striped waistcoat with matching trousers, a frilly pink shirt and a blue satin cloak. Do you know who Little Richard was?

Janet says, 'Come along John, we don't have all day. I want to get to the library before it closes!'

See John finish drying his nail varnish with a hairdryer. John is a popinjay.

Janet and John walk down the road to the bus

stop. Janet has to hold John's hand
to stop him skipping.

John likes skipping.

When they arrive in town Janet says, 'I'm going
to the library to get a medical dictionary, while
I'm gone, go to the delicatessen and pick up some
nice cheese for lunch. Do try to behave yourself!'

'I will,' says John.

John looks in all of the shop windows, just to see
his reflection, until he gets to the delicatessen.

Do you think 'delicatessen' is a funny word?

'Ding-a-ling' goes the shop bell.

See John look at all of the lovely cheeses. John
likes cheese.

'Hello John,' says Mrs Baxter. Mrs Baxter is
from Scotland. John has been to Scotland.

Mrs Baxter says, 'I'm just serving Mrs Oswald,
then I'll be right with you. I'm afraid I'm on my
own today as my assistant has the day off.'

John says, 'Would you like some help?' Kind
John.

Mrs Baxter says, 'Thank you John, that would be much appreciated.'

See John put on a white coat and hat in the stockroom.

Mrs Baxter says, 'Could you fetch a box of petticoat-tail biscuits from the cellar for Mrs Oswald please?'

'Of course,' says John. See John climb down the ladder and pass up the biscuits to Mrs Baxter.

Mrs Baxter says, 'While you're down there John, could you look to see if we have any more tins of Cullen Skink and barbecue relish in stock?'

John says, 'Yes, I can see a whole box of both of them, would you like me to bring some up?'

'Yes, thank you John,' says Mrs Baxter.

Do you know what Cullen Skink is? John doesn't, but thinks it might be a type of lizard. Silly John.

Soon, Mrs Oswald puts her shopping in her bag, pays Mrs Baxter and waves goodbye.

Mrs Baxter says, 'Thank you for your help today John. What was it you came in for?'

John says, 'I wanted to buy some cheese please.'

'Certainly,' says Mrs Baxter. 'We have a lovely, fresh, mature farmhouse Cheddar. As you've been such a help, you can have some, and a free tin of my best Mediterranean roasting rub.'

'Thank you,' says John. He waves goodbye to Mrs Baxter and hops and skips down the road to meet Janet.

When John arrives outside the library, Janet is waiting.

'Why are you so late John?' says Janet.

John says, 'I went to the delicatessen and saw Mrs Oswald and Mrs Baxter. I could see Mrs Baxter needed a pair of strong hands so I volunteered. She asked if I could pop downstairs and see if I could spot her Cullen Skink. I managed to lay hands on the box with relish and hand up Mrs Oswald's petticoat tails too. Mrs Baxter said

I'd been such a good boy that she gave me a Mediterranean rub under the counter.'

Do you know how many different injuries can be inflicted with a medical dictionary? John does.

Hear the screams.

Poor John.

Janet and John
Go Shopping

Today, Janet and John are going shopping.

Do you like shopping? John does. Shopping is John's second favourite thing after redcurrant jelly.

See John put on his best shopping clothes – a sparkly black matador costume, with a yellow frilly shirt and shiny black patent-leather shoes. John is a popinjay.

Janet says, 'Hurry up John or we'll miss the bus!'

Soon Janet and John catch the bus into town.

Janet has to slap John's legs as he keeps pushing his bus ticket up his nose. Silly John.

When they arrive at the shops Janet and John go into the big department store.

John is very excited. See the damp patch.

Janet says, 'I'm going to have a look around the kitchen department. Can I trust you to stay out of mischief?'

'Yes,' says John.

Janet says, 'I'll see you back here in half an hour.'

See John hop and skip down the aisle of the store.

John sees Mrs Steward. 'Hello Mrs Steward,' says John.

Mrs Steward is from Hampshire. See the sailors.

Mrs Steward says, 'That was nimble footwork John. Do you dance?'

John says, 'Only in front of the mirror at home.'

Mrs Steward says, 'I'm looking for some new

dancing shoes right now, but I am always on the lookout for dancers for our ballroom class.

I'm sure we could make a fine dancer of you. I can just see you dancing the mazurka. You already have the right costume.'

See John blush.

John waves goodbye to Mrs Steward and skips gaily to the men's fashion department.

John does not like any of the styles of clothes. John likes satin, silk and lace.

John sees Mrs Llewellyn struggling with a big box.

'Can I help you with that?' says John. Kind John.

Mrs Llewellyn says, 'Thank you John. I was hoping my husband would have been here by now. I left him buying some trousers. He waited for ages to get served. They are very busy here and could do with someone like you who knows how to look after a lady.'

See John blush again.

Soon Mr Llewellyn comes back and John trots back to meet Janet.

Janet has bought some new kitchen scissors.

'Hello Janet,' says John.

Janet says, 'Have you been a good boy?'

'Yes,' says John. 'I saw Mrs Llewellyn. She was complaining that her husband wasn't very well served in the trouser department and said that I looked like a man who knew how to treat a lady properly. Before that I saw Mrs Steward. She was after a nice pump and said she was always on the lookout for a partner with a nimble foot and good ballroom and asked if I'd like to come to her special club and learn how to mazurka.'

Do you know how to get scissors out of plastic packaging in under a second? Janet does.

See Janet chase John.

Run, John, run.

John Goes Out to Lunch

Today, John is going out for lunch with a producer.

Do you know what a producer does?

John dresses up especially for the occasion in a red leather catsuit with diamanté lapels and pockets, a white silk scarf and a sparkly gold floppy hat with a feather. See Danny La Rue.

Janet says, 'Have a nice time at work, and you'd better behave yourself today or there will be trouble.'

See John flinch.

John hops and skips down the road to the railway station and catches the train into London.

John works part-time as a junior traffic-boy at the BBC.

After John has done his work for the morning, he sees Alan outside his door.

Alan says, 'Are ye ready for a drink yet?'

Alan likes a drink. Paint Alan's nose red.

John picks up his handbag and walks down the stairs because the lift is out of order, then down the road to the wine bar.

Do you think 'Scuffles' is a funny name for a wine bar?

When they get inside, Alan seems to know everyone there.

See John looking at a card with lots of funny drinks on it.

Alan orders some gin, and John has a Sanatogen Sling.

They sit down at a table near the window next to a big group of ladies.

One of the ladies says, 'I'm Mrs Galvin, are you the stripper?'

'No,' says John. See John blush.

Alan says, 'I'll get ma kit off for money – in fact I'll do it for nothing.'

Hear the ladies laugh – what fun!

Another lady says, 'A fellow Scot I see.' She introduces herself as Mrs Phillips.

Mrs Galvin says, 'Will you join us for a drink? We've ordered lots of Chinese food too.'

By the time she has reached the word 'drink' Alan is sitting at their table. Thirsty Alan.

Mrs Phillips says, 'I have another job and this is my leaving do. You boys aren't to pay for any drinks as we already have a kitty from the office.'

John and Alan have lots to drink and John sings and dances and helps to pass around the dim sum that Mrs Galvin ordered.

See Mrs Phillips dance on the table.

After lunch, John and Alan walk back to the office holding on to each other in case they get lost.

John waves goodbye to Alan and catches the train home.

When John gets home, Janet is tidying up her desk and getting rid of some old statements and bills.

Janet says, 'You're late today. Did you have a nice lunch?'

'Yes,' says John. 'We had a lovely time. We went to a place that Alan knows and sat next to a big group of ladies. They thought I was a stripper. Alan wanted to take off all of his clothes. Mrs Galvin laid on the food and I decided to help out with a song and dance and hand round her dumplings. Then Mrs Phillips got up on the table and Alan and I helped ourselves to her kitty.'

See Janet feed John's beard into the paper shredder. Hear the screams.

Poor John.

John Goes to the Office Party

Today, John is going to the office Christmas party.

Everyone is allowed to go in their own clothes. John takes lots of games and toys with him and a cup and plate labelled with his name.

John puts on his best party clothes – a mauve lurex catsuit with mother-of-pearl sequins, a tiara and a feather boa. John is a fop and a dandy.

Janet says, 'You'll need a big coat John, it's very cold today.'

See John put on a pink fur coat with ermine lapels and pockets and put a big book in his pocket

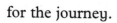

for the journey.

Janet says, 'Have a nice time at the party John, don't drink too much and do try to behave.'

See John wave goodbye as he hops and skips down the road.

John catches the train into London and soon arrives at the office.

On the way into the office, John sees John Humphrys. John Humphrys is a serious newsreader and works on Radio 4.

John used to work on Radio 4. Do you know what an 'incident' is? The Controller of Programmes does.

When John grows up he wants to be just like John Humphrys – only taller, not as Welsh and with less nose hair.

John goes into the newsroom and puts his toys and games in his desk. When he puts the lid down he notices that someone has written something rude on the lid. Do you know who

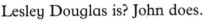

Lesley Douglas is? John does.

There is lots of music, food and fizzy drink. John's friend Alan has laid on all the food, but most of it is edible. See the empty amaretto bottles and Alan dancing with the coat stand.

Beryl-Ann is handing round the porridge vol-au-vents.

Soon it is time for the party games. Do you know how to play postman's knock? John doesn't.

See John giving people a pretend letter, then asking them for five pounds as it's Christmas.

Soon it is time for everyone to have a photograph taken. John has to stand at the back with the big boys. See how tall John is.

The small girls stand in the front. See Fran stand in front of John.

Fran says, 'What's that sticking in my back John?'

John says, 'Sorry about that, it's my thriller. I've just got to the exciting part.'

Fran says, 'It's quite a thick book, do you mind if I stand on it so that I am in the photograph?'

'Not at all,' says John, and puts the book on the floor so that Fran can stand on it. Kind John.

Soon it is time to go home. John puts his presents in his bag with his cards and a party bag with some cake and sweets.

When John arrives home, Janet is wrapping up some Christmas presents.

'Hello Janet,' says John.

'Did you have a nice time?' says Janet.

'Yes,' says John. 'There were lots of party games, music, food and drink. We all had our photograph taken. I was standing behind Fran when Fran said, "There's something sticking in my back." I said, "That's probably my Dick Francis." She asked if she could hop on to it for some photographs, that's why I have a funny look on my face.'

Do you know how to use up three rolls of

Sellotape, a ball of string and five rolls of wrapping paper in under two minutes?

Janet does.

See the big John-shaped present under the Christmas tree.

Poor John.

Janet and John
Go to the Village

Today, Janet and John are going to the village.

Janet has some books to take back to the library and John has to pay his pocket money into the post office.

John puts on his best shopping clothes – a silver and blue Regency-striped frock coat with gold buttons and blue braid, a frilly shirt, knee breeches and court shoes with white stockings. John is a dandy.

After John has finished with his electric beard straighteners, Janet and John walk down the lane to catch the bus into the village.

Do you like catching the bus? John does, but Janet has to put John's reins on to stop him crawling on the dirty floor.

When they arrive in the village, Janet says, 'You run along to the post office and I'll see you outside the library in half an hour.'

See John wave goodbye to Janet and hop and skip all the way to the post office.

'Ding-a-ling' goes the bell on the post-office door.

There is quite a long queue in the post office. John stands in the queue behind Mrs Katcherian.

'Hello Mrs Katcherian,' says John.

'Hello John,' says Mrs Katcherian.

What fun!

Mrs Katcherian says, 'I see you in here every week John, are you saving up for something special?'

John says, 'No, I just like writing down all of

the numbers on paper, then adding them all up.'

Mrs Katcherian says, 'You should really try to use double-entry bookkeeping, it's a very good way of balancing your income and expenditure. You could have a trial balance every day.'

See John stand on one leg.

John says, 'I'm not very good at balancing.'

Silly John.

Mrs Katcherian says, 'You should call around when my husband is in, he explains bookkeeping, asset revaluation and inflation much better than I do.'

'Thank you,' says John.

Soon John gets to the front of the queue.

'Hello John,' says Mrs Martin. 'Are you just paying in your pocket money?'

'Yes,' says John, 'but I am waiting for a parcel too.'

Mrs Martin says, 'What sort of parcel is it

you are waiting for?'

John says, 'It's a replacement organ stop for my second trumpet. The old one came loose last week when I was practising some Willcocks.'

Mrs Martin says, 'I'll keep an eye out for it John and deliver it personally as soon as it comes in.'

Kind Mrs Martin.

Once John has paid in his pocket money, he skips gaily back to the library to meet Janet.

Janet is already waiting.

Janet has just borrowed a big cookbook from the library.

Janet says, 'Did you behave today John?'

John says, 'Yes, I saw Mrs Katcherian. She said that once she'd examined the assets and taken care of inflation I could come around and see her when her husband was at home and they'd show me how to do double entry.

'Then I saw Mrs Martin. I told her that I was

waiting for a replacement for a loose trumpet and once I'd described the knob she said my package would be safe in her hands and that she'd take care of it personally when she was on her rounds.'

See Janet boil.

See John run.

Can you hit a fleeing newsreader with a large cookbook?

Janet can.

Poor John

John Goes to the Office

Today, John is going into work.

John has a part-time job at the BBC.

Do you know what John does at work?

John puts on his special work clothes – a pink satin suit with magenta lapels, buttons and pockets, a sparkly pink handbag and knee-high orange platform boots. John is a fop.

After John has done his traffic-boy work for the day, he hops and skips down the road towards the train station.

On the way, John sees a sign advertising a Scottish wildlife exhibition.

Do you like wildlife? John does.

John is very excited. See the damp patch.

See John go up the steps into the exhibition.

John looks at lots of pictures of birds.

John likes birds, but they always go after his plums.

While John is looking at a stuffed bird in a case, a man with a name badge that reads 'Mr Bantick' says, 'That's a bittern. We don't have them any more in Scotland, but I can show you lots of pictures of birds we do have.'

Kind Mr Bantick.

John says, 'Yes please.'

Mr Bantick gets them both a cup of tea and tells John all about rearing birds of prey.

Mr Bantick says, 'If you come to one of our centres you can handle them too.'

John says, 'What do they eat?'

Mr Bantick says, 'When we breed them in captivity, they eat chicken.'

John says, 'If I come to Scotland, will I be safe if I am walking down the road eating a chicken sandwich?'

See tea come out of Mr Bantick's nose.

Mr Bantick says, 'If you go over to see Mrs Evans she will take your picture with the imprint of the bird of your choice in the background and make it look like a stamp.'

See John skip over to see Mrs Evans. What fun!

John can't decide whether he prefers a stork or an Arctic tern.

Mrs Evans says, 'You could always have a bearded tit.'

See John scowl.

Mrs Evans says, 'If you have the stork first we can do the Arctic tern afterwards, but I have to go downstairs shortly to set up the crustacean exhibit. We have live lobsters, crayfish and crabs in tanks.'

Soon it is time for John's train.

See John wave goodbye to Mr Bantick and Mrs

Evans and walk to the station.

When John gets home, Janet is making some pancakes.

Janet says, 'Did you have a nice day at work John?'

'Yes,' says John. 'On the way home, I saw a man who was very interested in wildlife. Mr Bantick was showing me pictures of some of his birds and said that I could handle some of them if I wanted, but told me that I wouldn't get bittern as the one he had that morning had already been stuffed.

'Then Mrs Evans took a picture of me with a stork on. She told me that she'd be happy to let me have a tern later but she was in a hurry as she had crabs downstairs.'

Can you put a big dent in a hot frying pan?

Janet can.

Hear the screams.

Poor John.

Janet and John
Go Christmas Shopping

Today, Janet and John are going into town to collect some Christmas decorations.

John is very excited. See the damp patch.

John changes his pull-ups and puts on his special Christmas-shopping clothes – a red velvet suit with white fur trimmings on the pockets, black patent-leather boots and a long red cloak with sequins on it.

John is a popinjay.

Janet has to put on John's reins to stop him running all the way.

When they arrive at the shops there are lots of people queuing up to buy tinsel and decorations.

John keeps crawling on the floor and getting in people's way, so Janet says, 'Why don't you go outside and look at the Christmas lights? I'll see you back here in half an hour. Do try to behave!'

'I will,' says John, and hops and skips along the road.

Outside the pet-grooming shop John sees Mrs Bickerdyke.

Mrs Bickerdyke is from Yorkshire. See the chimneys.

Mrs Bickerdyke says, 'Eh-up Fluffywhiskers.'

Mrs Bickerdyke has her little dog with her.

John likes dogs.

Mrs Bickerdyke says, 'I'm just going to get Trixie's coat clipped, would you like to come in to watch the dogs being groomed?'

'Yes please,' says John.

Mrs Mayhew, who owns the shop, has lots of

dogs to shampoo and clip their coats.

John says, 'You are very busy Mrs Mayhew, do you do all breeds of dogs?'

Mrs Mayhew says, 'Yes I do John, but mostly the long-haired breeds. Tomorrow I have a lot of people booked in from the local spaniel breeders. They are very nice to work with. I have a Brittany spaniel to do first thing, a springer spaniel after that and then a cocker spaniel just after lunch. You could always pop in to give me a hand. I can see you are very good with your own hair.'

See John blush. Paint John's face red.

Soon it is time for John to meet Janet. See John wave goodbye to all his friends and skip gaily along the road to meet Janet.

Janet has bought lots of tinsel, some pretty glass baubles, some fairy lights and a big pointed star for the tree.

Janet says, 'Did you behave John?'

John says, 'Yes, I did. I saw Mrs Bickerdyke,

she was just going to get her Trixie trimmed. Mrs Mayhew asked me if I wanted to watch. She said that she is very busy just before Christmas and gets a lot of special requests. She said that if I want to pop back on Saturday I can watch her do a Brittany first thing, springer later in the morning and cocker after lunch.'

Hear Janet grind her teeth and hiss.

See Janet tie John up with the fairy lights.

Can you insert a large sparkly star in a struggling newsreader? Janet can.

Hear the screams.

Poor John.

John Goes to the Office Christmas Party

Today, John is going to the office Christmas party.

See John put on his best party clothes – a pink satin frock coat with orange sparkly tights, a bright green frilly shirt and a yellow floppy hat with a feather. John is a dandy.

Janet says, 'If that Dedicoat fellow is going, you are not to sit next to him again. It took me weeks to get the piccalilli stains out of your trousers. Will you try to behave this year?'

'I will,' says John.

When John arrives at the office, he sees his

friend Alan from the newsroom. Alan is from Wealdstone but likes to pretend that he lives in Harrow.

'Hello Alan,' says John.

Alan says, 'We've decided to have the Christmas party at a local restaurant this year as Mr Shennon got a bit cross last time after the photocopier was full of red hair.'

John says, 'Yes, it was probably from Lynn's Tickle Me Elmo.'

Alan says, 'We're meeting downstairs at twelve o'clock. Don't be late.'

'I won't,' says John.

At twelve o'clock, everyone meets outside the office and they walk around the corner to the restaurant. Do you like Indian food? Alan does. See the stains.

At the door of the restaurant they are greeted by Miss Shah, the owner's daughter. She takes their coats and directs them to a big table.

Once everyone is settled down, Miss Shah

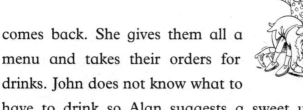

comes back. She gives them all a menu and takes their orders for drinks. John does not know what to have to drink so Alan suggests a sweet yogurt drink called lassi.

Alan orders a mutton jihad, Beryl-Ann wants a chicken fatwa, Lynn wants a pie with curry sauce and Terry and Charles decide to share a Wogan josh.

John does not know what to order. See John blub.

Miss Shah says, 'There, there, don't worry, we have a special dish that my brother Goldan prepares that has lots of small samples of all of the main courses. Would you like to try that?'

'Yes please,' says John.

Soon the food begins to arrive. There are poppadoms, naan bread, chapattis and lots of rice dishes.

Alan says to John, 'If you want to make it really authentic, you have to lay on the floor with a bowl

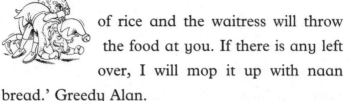

of rice and the waitress will throw the food at you. If there is any left over, I will mop it up with naan bread.' Greedy Alan.

See John gobble down his food. Miss Shah says, 'Is your meal alright John?'

'Yes,' says John, 'but I didn't enjoy this side dish as I don't like peas very much.'

Miss Shah says, 'Not everyone likes the aloo dishes, I will take them away.'

Kind Miss Shah.

Soon everyone has finished their meal, Alan and Lynn have finished dancing on the table and Charles and Beryl-Ann are asking the other people in the restaurant if they know the answer to the Glasgow pub-quiz question 'Are you lookin' at me?' Terry is asleep. See Terry dribble.

John waves goodbye to his friends and hops and skips all the way to the railway station to catch the train home.

When John gets home, Janet is putting up the

Christmas tree. Janet says, 'Did you have a nice time John?'

'Yes,' says John. 'I had a sweet lassi on the table, which made a nice change, but Alan said that it would be best if I lay on the floor with a pilau to properly enjoy the Goldan Shah special. Alan said he'd help to mop it up with his naan. I rather enjoyed it as it was nice and hot. There was one thing I didn't care for and the lady who was serving me said she never bothered with aloo either and that hot peas were not everyone's cup of tea.'

Can you insert a six-foot spruce into a fast-moving newsreader? Janet can.

Hear the screams.

Poor John.

Janet and John Go Fashion Shopping

Today, Janet and John are going to the shops to buy some clothes.

John likes going shopping for clothes. John is very fashionable.

See John get dressed in his purple frock coat, his shirt with the frilly collar and his blue silk trousers with gold brocade.

Janet likes to go shopping for clothes with John. Janet sees John get his wallet out. See the moths.

See Janet and John go into an accessories shop.

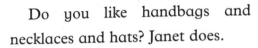

Do you like handbags and necklaces and hats? Janet does.

John likes sparkly things too. See John look at some lovely silver, green and gold beads.

John goes to talk to the shop assistant. The shop assistant is called Becky. Are you called Becky? Nearly everyone else is.

Clever John reads her name badge. Becky is drinking a can of pop and eating a very big cake.

Becky has a wobbly white tummy that sticks out over the top of her trousers. Lots of girls have these. They are very fashionable.

'Can you tell me what these are?' says John, holding up the beads.

Becky is eating her cake. 'Bag charms,' says Becky. Becky talks with her mouth full. See John brush off the cake crumbs.

John asks, 'Do you have a changing room?'

'What d'you want a changing room for?' says

Becky. See Becky take a big bite of her cake and a swig of pop.

'I want to try them on,' says John.

Can you squirt pop out of your nose? Becky can.

Do you know what the Heimlich manoeuvre is? John does. Lucky Becky.

See John standing behind Becky with his arms around her waist. John has long arms.

See Janet come back to see what the noise is.

See John drop Becky on the floor and put his arms behind his back.

Janet says, 'I leave you alone for five minutes . . .' and gets out her umbrella.

See John run.

Silly John has left his wallet on the counter. See Janet smile.

Janet and John Go to a Barbecue

Today, it has stopped raining for a few hours and Janet and John are going to a barbecue.

Do you like barbecues? John does.

Janet says, 'You'd better put on some old clothes John as you do tend to get covered in splashes of sauce when you eat.'

See John put on a seventeenth-century black velvet frock coat with red trimmings and flowery black and white lapels, matching knee breeches, white socks and a white frilly shirt with a black silk cravat. John is king of the fops.

Janet says, 'I have to go to the off-licence and pick up some wine. You can pop along to the butcher's shop and pick up some meat, nothing too fancy mind. I'll meet you at the party.'

Janet gives John some money and John hops and skips gaily down the lane to the butcher's shop.

'Ding-a-ling' goes the shop bell.

Mr Ware the butcher says, 'Hello John, what can I get for you today?'

John says, 'I'd like to buy some meat for a barbecue.'

Mr Ware says, 'Well, pork spare ribs are the best-selling cut for barbecues, but lots of other cuts of meat work just as well. Some of my customers like to use fillet steak, but it's quite expensive. Ox tongue is nearly as good and a lot cheaper, I could let you have quite a lot of that for not too much money. It's best if you marinate it in a little wine, or something similar, for a few minutes before you cook it.'

'Thank you,' says John. John likes a bargain.

John pays Mr Ware and then trips down the road swinging his bag.

When John arrives at the barbecue he sees Mrs Aguilar. Mrs Aguilar is from Texas – see the wide open spaces.

'Hello Mrs Aguilar,' says John.

'Hello John,' says Mrs Aguilar. What fun!

Mrs Aguilar says, 'Did you bring some meat for the barbecue?'

'Yes,' says John, and shows Mrs Aguilar the bag.

Mrs Aguilar says, 'I hope you brought some steak. We know how to cook a steak in Texas.'

John says, 'I brought some spare ribs and some ox tongue.'

Mrs Aguilar says, 'I'm OK with the ribs, but I don't rightly like the sound of eating a tongue.'

John says, 'The butcher told me that it is as good as fillet steak.'

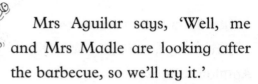

Mrs Aguilar says, 'Well, me and Mrs Madle are looking after the barbecue, so we'll try it.'

John says, 'Mr Ware, the butcher, said we should marinate it in wine for a while before cooking it.'

Mrs Aguilar says, 'Well, we have some dry cider we've been using for the sauce, we'll give that a try if you can help.'

See John put on an apron and get the meat out.

When John has finished the marinade, he washes his hands and gets some plates ready.

Soon Mrs Aguilar has finished cooking the first of the ox tongue and tries some with John.

John quite likes it, but Mrs Aguilar says, 'It's delicious John.'

John sees Janet coming through the gate with two bottles of wine.

'Hello Janet,' says John.

Janet says, 'Who was that woman I saw you talking to?'

See the warning signs.

John says, 'That was Mrs Aguilar. She was congratulating me on my prowess with the meat. We were just trying my hot tongue in cider before you arrived. She loved it and was surprised afterwards when I was indifferent.'

Can you pull a fully grown newsreader through a hawthorn hedge by his beard?

Janet can.

Hear the screams.

Poor John.

Janet and John Go Cruising

Today, Janet and John are going on holiday on a cruise ship.

See John put on the clothes he wears every time he goes cruising.

John puts on a black velvet frock coat with red trimmings and black and white lapels, matching knee breeches, white socks, a white frilly shirt with a red lace ruff and cuffs and a matching red hat with a feather on it.

John is a popinjay.

Janet straps John into his safety seat and gives him a barley sugar for the journey and they drive to the docks.

When they arrive in the car park John helps Janet unload the seventeen cases of clothes he has brought for the trip.

While the bags are being put on a trolley, John refreshes his make-up as his lipstick has smudged because of the sweets. Messy John.

Janet and John follow the signs to embarkation and while Janet is queuing, John hops and skips up and down the dock swinging his handbag.

When they get on board, there is a champagne reception. Do you like champagne? John does, but he is not allowed to have more than two glasses or he goes all floppy.

After they have finished their drinks, Janet says, 'I'm going to the cabin now as I'm quite tired after the long drive. I'll meet you for lunch by the entrance to the ballroom in an hour. Do try to behave!'

'I will,' says John.

See John walk up the main staircase to the promenade deck.

Do you know what a promenade is? John thinks that it is a lobster dish. Silly John.

While John is practising his best salty sea-dog walk, he sees Mrs Bickerdyke.

'Eh-up Fluffywhiskers,' says Mrs Bickerdyke. Mrs Bickerdyke is from Yorkshire – see Geoffrey Boycott.

Mrs Bickerdyke says, 'Nice to see you on the trip again this year. Have you brought enough clothes this time? I'm sure I saw you wear the same outfit for three hours last year.' Funny Mrs Bickerdyke.

John says, 'Yes thank you, I have seventeen cases this time. Are you going to be in the cabaret this year?'

Mrs Bickerdyke says, 'Not this time. For the last year I have been doing these corporate stress-management courses for some of these soft London types who don't know what a hard day's graft is.

It's astonishing what you can get away with on these things. I had some of the last lot doing role play with glove puppets. I brought my SpongeBob puppet with me just in case. You're more than welcome to play with it if you want. I'm off to the bingo now, so I'll see thee later.'

See John wave goodbye to Mrs Bickerdyke and hop and skip along the deck.

John sees Melanie Frontage.

'Hello Johnny,' says Mrs Frontage.

'Hello Mrs Frontage,' says John. What fun!

Melanie Frontage has a special shop selling helpful things for married people. See the black windows.

John says, 'I didn't know you liked cruises.'

Melanie Frontage says, 'Yes, I have some friends in the crew. I am really looking forward to the dinner on Wednesday as they have a special big seafood supper with lots of winkles.'

Do you like winkles? Melanie Frontage does.

John says, 'I like the food, but the drinks are very expensive.'

Melanie Frontage says, 'Yes, they are. I always bring my own bottle of Grand Marnier in my bag and top up my glass under the table. You are more than welcome to join me for a drink at dinner if you like.'

'Thank you,' says John.

Soon it is time to meet Janet for lunch. See John skip gaily down the stairs to the ballroom.

Soon, Janet arrives. Janet says, 'Have you been a good boy?'

'Yes,' says John. 'I saw Mrs Bickerdyke. She was telling me all about a new service she's providing. She does executive relief with a SpongeBob glove puppet and said I'd be welcome to try it out later. Then I saw Melanie Frontage. She said that she had friends in the crew and was looking forward to trying the huge winkle supper and said that if I wanted, I could join her for dinner and liquor under the table.'

See Janet dangle John over the side of the ship by his ears.

Paint John's ears red.

Poor John.

John Goes for a Ride on his Scooter

Today, it has stopped raining for a while and John is going for a ride on his scooter.

Janet says, 'Make sure you take a waterproof with you as it might rain later on.'

See John put on a pink shiny rain suit with orange and purple spots and his best gold wellingtons.

John is a popinjay.

Janet says, 'Don't be too long, we're having bubble and squeak for lunch.'

Do you like bubble and squeak?

John likes it with redcurrant jelly. John has

redcurrant jelly with nearly everything.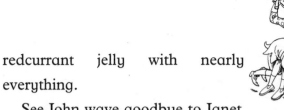

See John wave goodbye to Janet and scoot as fast as he can down the lane. See how fast John can go!

When John gets to the end of the lane he stops by the side of the main road. John knows the Green Cross Code.

Clever John.

As John is waiting to cross the road, he sees Mrs Belbin painting her summer house in the garden.

'Hello Mrs Belbin,' says John.

'Hello John,' says Mrs Belbin. What fun!

John says, 'That's a pretty colour pink. I have some trousers in exactly that shade.'

'Yes it is a pretty shade,' says Mrs Belbin. 'I couldn't stand the purple that my husband painted it last year, so I thought I'd do it while he is out playing golf.'

John says, 'Would you like me to give you a hand?'

'Yes please,' says Mrs Belbin. 'I'd like to get it done before the rain comes back. I will have to redo some of it because the milkman put his fingerprints on the door when he called this morning.'

See John park his scooter and hop and skip through the gate into the garden.

Mrs Belbin gives John a brush. See John put lots of paint on the brush. See paint drip on to Mrs Belbin's shoes.

John says, 'Sorry Mrs Belbin.'

'Don't worry,' says Mrs Belbin. 'They are only an old pair. The trick is not to put too much paint on the brush or to press too hard, otherwise the purple shows through.'

Soon the summer house is finished and Mrs Belbin says, 'Thank you John. Can I get you some tea and something to eat?'

John says, 'Yes please! But I don't want to spoil my lunch, so only a little.'

Mrs Belbin says, 'I made some game pie at the

weekend, there is a small piece left as long as you don't mind pheasant and hare.'

John says, 'That would be very nice.'

See John go into the kitchen and sit at the table to drink his tea and eat some pie.

Soon it is time to go back for lunch. See John wipe the crumbs from his beard, wave goodbye to Mrs Belbin and scoot back up the lane.

When John gets home, Janet is cooking lunch.

Janet says, 'Did you have a nice time John?'

John says, 'Yes, I did. When I got to the end of the lane, I saw Mrs Belbin in the garden. She was freshening up her gazebo while her husband was out. She showed me where the milkman had put his hand that morning and said that if I gave her a hand, a delicate touch was needed and the grip was very important otherwise it would end up purple rather than pink. I got a bit too excited and made a mess of her shoes. Then she let me have a bit of hare pie in the kitchen.'

See Janet sit John on the cooker.
See John bubble and squeak.
Poor John.

Janet and John Go to the Sports Centre

Janet goes to the sports centre twice a week for her kendo classes. Do you know what kendo is?

John doesn't. John thinks that kendo is a type of Japanese coffee. Silly John.

John puts on his sparkly green shell suit with gold piping, bright yellow trainers and his best Dora the Explorer sports bag. John is a dandy.

Janet puts her armour in the car and tells John to hurry up.

See Janet strap John into his safety seat in the car. Janet says, 'As it's raining today, did you

 remember to pack your colouring book and pencils so that you have something to do while I'm in class?'

'Yes, I did,' says John.

When they get to the sports centre, Janet unpacks her armour and says, 'I'll see you in the café in an hour – do try to behave.'

'I will,' says John.

While John is watching one of the aerobics classes from the foyer, he sees Mrs Wallis. 'Hello John,' says Mrs Wallis. 'Are you here for the over-sixties fitness class?'

'No,' says John, 'I would get all hot and sweaty and I've just washed and curled my hair.'

Mrs Wallis says, 'Perhaps you would like to have a look around the gym? Exercise is very good for people of all ages. Here is Mrs Cornwell who takes the classes now. I'm sure she would be able to suggest some exercises you might enjoy.'

Do you know how to look sceptical? John does.

When they get to the gym, Mrs Cornwell says,

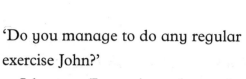

'Do you manage to do any regular exercise John?'

John says, 'I sometimes play on the swings and climbing frame, but it's too wet today.'

Mrs Cornwell says, 'All of the ladies here like to see men with a bit of muscle. Let me show you some of the machines we use. This one is very good for exercising your deltoids John. Do you know what the deltoids are?'

John says, 'Yes, but I'm not allowed to watch *Doctor Who* in case I get nightmares and wet the bed.'

Mrs Cornwell says, 'The pull-up machine is very good for your triceps. I'm just going to get changed. You can watch Mrs Wallis using the dumb-bells to do an arm exercise called "curls".'

John says, 'I have some heated rollers that do mine.' Silly John.

Mrs Wallis says, 'I always look forward to my gym sessions as it's a nice feeling afterwards when your muscles are pumped up. I try to get at least

two sessions a week, or three if I can get someone to hold the fort at work.'

Soon it is time for John to meet Janet. See John wave goodbye to the ladies and hop and skip back to the café.

When Janet arrives, she says, 'Did you behave John?'

'Yes,' says John. 'I saw Mrs Wallis. She said I should go with her to see Mrs Cornwell as it might be good for me. Mrs Cornwell showed me her pull-ups, and while she was getting changed I saw Mrs Wallis's curls. She said she always looks forward to getting pumped and comes at least twice a week or three times if she can get someone to cover her. Mrs Cornwell said that I should come back regularly as all of the ladies like to see a man with a big chest, and love muscle.'

See Janet fetch her wooden practice sword.

See John run.

Run, John, run.

John Goes to Church

Today, John is going to church to practise his organ.

John likes to play the organ. See John's powerful glasses.

Janet says, 'Hurry up John! You've tried on ten outfits already. You're going to be late again and the wrestling starts in ten minutes.'

Do you like wrestling? Janet does.

John puts on a lime-green velvet suit with embroidered gold treble clefs on the lapels, a yellow frilly shirt and a bright orange sparkly bow tie.

John is a popinjay

When John gets to the church he sees Pastor Kidneys.

'Hello John,' says Pastor Kidneys. 'I hope you don't mind, but Mrs Dowell has brought the choir in for an extra practice.'

John says, 'I don't mind at all. I like playing with a choir.'

See John wave goodbye to Pastor Kidneys and hop and skip into the church.

John sees Mrs Dowell. 'Hello Mrs Dowell,' says John.

Mrs Dowell is from Bristol.

Mrs Dowell says, 'Have you come about the advertisement I put in the newsletter for male choristers?'

'No,' says John, 'I have come to practise my organ playing.'

Mrs Dowell says, 'That's a shame, I have a lot of ladies in the choir but I am really keen to get a few more men involved. If you or anyone you

know is interested, I'm desperate for a good male tenor.'

John says, 'I sometimes sing along to my Liberace records, but I am usually busy playing the organ.'

Mrs Dowell says, 'Do you know Handel's *Messiah*? There are a few excerpts that I'd like to run through, particularly "Promise and Fulfilment". Perhaps you could play for us?'

'Yes, I have the music in my bag,' says John. What fun!

See John hop and skip over to the organ and get out his music.

Hear John play the organ while the choir joins in. Clever John.

When choir practice has finished, Mrs Dowell thanks John for playing and asks if he would play for them again next week.

'Yes please,' says John.

When John gets home, Janet is watching the wrestling. Janet likes wrestling.

Janet says, 'Did you have a good practice John?'

'Yes,' says John. 'Mrs Dowell was very impressed with my Handel. She asked me if I would like to play "Promise and Fulfilment". She said that she's always interested in male members. She said that she was desperate and that if I was interested, she would do anything for a tenor and would be delighted if I could come out to play next week.'

Do you know what a gorilla press powerslam is?

Janet does.

Hear the screams.

Poor John.

John Goes to the Grocer's

Today, John is going to the grocer's shop in the village.

Janet says, 'Hurry up John, or the shop will be closed by the time you get there.'

John says, 'I'm just waiting for my fake tan to dry otherwise it will stain my frilly shirt collar.'

John is a fop.

When John has finished his make-up, Janet gives John a list of things to buy and some money.

Janet says, 'Don't be too long, I have my new weights bench being delivered and need a hand moving some boxes so that there is space to set it up.'

Do you like weight training? Janet does.

See John wave goodbye to Janet and hop and skip gaily down the road swinging his sparkly blue shopping bag.

When John arrives in the village, he gets the list and the money out of his best Dora the Explorer purse and skips into the grocer's shop. 'Ding-a-ling' goes the shop bell.

Mrs Trott says, 'Good morning John, what can I do for you today?'

As John puts the list on the counter the back doorbell rings, 'ding-dong'.

Mrs Trott says, 'That will be the man with the new pull-out storage units for my hot cabinet. Why don't you come around and get what you need while I'm dealing with the driver?'

'Thank you,' says John.

See John standing behind the till playing at being a shopkeeper.

While John is putting his shopping on the counter, Mrs Booth comes into the shop.

Mrs Booth says, 'I didn't know you worked here John.'

John says, 'I'm just helping out as Mrs Trott is busy.'

See Mrs Booth get out a long shopping list and put it on the counter.

Mrs Booth says, 'Do you know if you have apricots in stock?'

John says, 'I'll have a look.' See John go to the room at the back of the shop and look at all the tins.

John says, 'We don't seem to do apricots in stock, but we do have them in syrup or fruit juice if that's alright?'

Silly John.

Mrs Booth says, 'I have quite a list of things to get as I am trying out some new recipes, so it might be quicker if I come and have a look for

myself if you don't mind?'

'Not at all,' says John. See John take Mrs Booth through to the storeroom.

Mrs Booth says, 'Would you mind getting down that box of cereal from the top shelf and the porridge next to it, as I can't quite reach?'

'Of course,' says John. See how tall John is.

When Mrs Booth has all she needs, John gives Mrs Trott a hand to bring in the new equipment for the hot cabinet.

Kind John.

Soon it is time for John to go. John puts his shopping in his bag, waves goodbye to the ladies and hops and skips all the way home – what fun!

When John arrives, Janet is using her new weight bench.

'You were gone a long time,' says Janet.

John says, 'Mrs Trott was quite busy and asked if I would help out as she was expecting a man to come with her new hot drawers and needed

someone to help. Mrs Booth had
a big list of things she wanted to
try out. I was up to the apricots
with her on the counter, but she had to go into the
storeroom to make sure she got her oats and hand
down her Shreddies.'

Can you lift a fully grown traffic boy over your
head? Janet can.

Poor John.

Janet and John
Go to a Plant Sale

Today, Janet and John are going to a plant sale at the vicarage.

Do you like gardening? Janet does, but John mostly makes mud pies, paints snails and collects worms.

See John put on a pink and orange flowered white satin suit with a bright green silk shirt and a matching beret.

John is a dandy.

As soon as John has taken his heated rollers out and put on his hairspray, Janet puts on John's reins to stop him jumping in all the puddles as they walk down the lane.

When they arrive at the vicarage, there are lots of people already there. Janet says, 'I'm going to help with the refreshments, do try to stay out of trouble.'

'I will,' says John.

See John hop and skip gaily around the plant displays.

John sees Mrs Scott-Smith.

'Hello Mrs Scott-Smith,' says John.

Mrs Scott-Smith is from Cornwall. See Rick Stein.

Mrs Scott-Smith says, 'Hello John. Have you seen my husband at all? He went off ages ago to look for a *Clematis montana* for the garden wall. It's so dull in the spring and I want something exciting that will add a splash of colour.'

John says, 'No, I haven't seen your husband, but I did notice some clematis on one of the displays. I'll show you where they are.' Kind John.

While John is showing Mrs Scott-Smith where to find the clematis, John sees Pastor Kidneys.

Pastor Kidneys is talking to Mr and Mrs Plumb. Mr and Mrs Plumb are from Yorkshire. See the chimneys.

Pastor Kidneys says, 'That's rather a splendid *Streptosolen jamesonii* you have there Mrs Plumb, I wonder if I might take a picture of it for the parish magazine?'

Mrs Plumb says, 'Yes, of course, perhaps Peter and John could hold these pots of *Ranunculus asiaticus* while I arrange it so it can be seen properly?'

See John and Mr Plumb take the pots while the photograph is taken.

After the photograph is taken, John sees the refreshment stall where Janet is working. The refreshment stall is selling ice cream. Do you like

ice cream? John does. See the bingo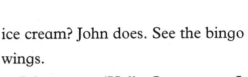
wings.

John says, 'Hello Janet, can I
have some ice cream please?'

Janet says, 'Just a small one, as you haven't
had your lunch yet. Have you been a good boy?'

'Yes,' says John. 'I saw Mrs Scott-Smith. She
said she wanted something exciting against the
garden wall and had sent her husband off. But as
he was having trouble finding the clematis, I
helped her out. Then I saw Mrs Plumb. She asked
if her husband and I could hold a buttercup each
while she had a photograph taken of her
marmalade bush for the parish magazine.'

See Janet push a big container of ice cream on
to John's head.

Poor John.

Janet and John Go to the Supermarket

Today, Janet and John are going to the supermarket.

John puts on his best shopping clothes – a pink velvet suit with a white frilly shirt, a pink cravat and a matching hat and wristwatch. John is a popinjay.

Janet says, 'Come along John or we'll miss the bus.'

See John quickly finish putting on his false eyelashes.

When Janet and John arrive in town Janet says,

'Do you want to come to the shop with me or would you prefer to play on the slide and swings?'

Do you like swinging? John does.

John says, 'I'd like to go to the playground please.'

Janet says, 'Right, I'll meet you when I've done the shopping. Try not to get into mischief!'

'I will,' says John.

See John hop and skip over to the playground.

When John arrives at the playground all of the swings are being used, so John goes on the slide.

See John come down the slide backwards. Silly John.

See John fall off of the slide. See John blub.

Mrs Fagen from the playgroup picks John up and dusts him off.

Mrs Fagen says, 'Oh dear, I think you have broken your watch too.'

See John blub again.

Mrs Fagen says, 'There is a jeweller's just

around the corner, why don't you see if they can fix it?'

John thanks Mrs Fagen and trots over to the jeweller's.

'Ding-a-ling' goes the shop bell.

John sees Mrs Mason. 'Hello Mrs Mason,' says John.

Mrs Mason is from Liverpool. See the funny church.

Mrs Mason says, 'I see you've broken your watch. Let me see if I can fix it for you.'

John says, 'The glass is broken and there is a big scratch on the face and both of the hands are bent.'

Mrs Mason says, 'I see you've grazed your hand too. I used to be a nurse. I'll put some ointment on it for you.'

Mrs Mason looks in her workshop and says, 'I think I have some parts that will fit this watch. We sell and repair Citizen watches, but I don't get many in pink!'

Mrs Mason goes to the back of the shop while John dries his trousers near the radiator.

Soon Mrs Mason has repaired John's watch. John pays Mrs Mason and hops and skips gaily back to the playground.

When John arrives, Janet is waiting.

Janet says, 'Where have you been?'

John says, 'I had an accident. I fell off the slide and damaged my pink Citizen. Mrs Fagen had a quick look and said that she knew a lady who used to be a nurse who could help. Mrs Mason said that it would need two hands and a face put on it before it would work properly again. She did it all in a few minutes and only charged me twenty pounds.'

Can you roar like a bull elephant?

Janet can.

See John run. Run, John, run.

Janet and John
Go into Town

Today, Janet and John are going to the shops in Uckfield. John likes going shopping.

See John put on his best shopping clothes – a sparkly yellow sequinned catsuit with a red cape, red leather boots and a gold handbag. John is a fop.

As soon as John has finished drying his nail varnish, they are ready to go. See John skip all the way down the lane to the bus stop.

When they arrive in the village, Janet says, 'We have to go to the department store to pick up some new roasting tins.'

Do you like a roast dinner? John does. See the redcurrant jelly.

See John swinging around every lamp post as they walk down the high street. See Janet pull John's ear.

Paint John's ear red.

When they arrive at the department store Janet says, 'You can either come to the kitchenware department with me, or have a look around – as long as you behave.'

'I will,' says John.

Janet says, 'I'll see you by the entrance, and no going the wrong way up and down the escalators either.'

Can you pull a face when someone isn't looking? John can.

See John looking around at all of the different departments in the store. What fun!

John goes into the flooring department and bounces up and down on the big rolls of carpet.

John sees Mrs Duff. 'Hello Mrs Duff,' says John.

Mrs Duff is from Glasgow. See the traffic congestion.

Mrs Duff says, 'Please, call me Wilma. I see you like some of the long-fibre carpets.'

'Yes,' says John. 'It's very soft and comfortable.'

Mrs Duff says, 'This one is on special offer this week. It's very hard-wearing and perfect for a sitting room. The other things we have on offer at the moment are our rectangular rugs. They really help to provide a point of interest in the room. If you look under the dining table over there, you will see what I mean.'

While John is looking at all of the lovely carpets, Mr Duff comes in.

'Hello John,' says Mr Duff.

Mr Duff says, 'I see my wife has got you interested in the carpets, they are very decorative and really easy to put down, but if they don't appeal she will show you some rather nice

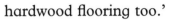

hardwood flooring too.'

'Thank you,' says John. 'I will speak to Janet about it.'

See John wave goodbye to Mr and Mrs Duff and skip gaily back to meet Janet.

Soon Janet arrives. Janet has bought three big roasting tins.

Janet says, 'Have you been a good boy?'

'Yes,' says John. 'I saw Mrs Duff. She was showing me a very attractive rectangular rug under the table and was just suggesting a long shag in the sitting room when Mr Duff came in and said that if I wanted something attractive and surprisingly easy to lay, she would do a great job. He told me that if I wasn't interested, I probably need flooring.'

See Janet go purple.

See Janet put big dents in the new roasting tins.

Hear the screams.

Poor John.

Janet and John Go to a Firework Display

Today, Janet and John are going to a firework display.

Do you like fireworks? John does.

See John putting on his best Guy Fawkes costume – silver and black doublet with green hose, a starched ruff and a black hat with an ostrich feather.

John is a popinjay.

Janet says that Guy Fawkes was the last man to enter Parliament with honest intent. Funny Janet.

John is very excited, so Janet packs some extra pull-ups and John's best Tellytubbies changing mat.

See Janet put on John's reins to stop him skipping all the way to the park.

When they arrive, it is quite early and the display is still being set up.

Janet sees Mrs Madle from the Women's Institute.

Janet says, 'I'm just going to talk to Mrs Madle. She is making the toffee apples.'

Do you like toffee apples? John does.

Janet says, 'Can I trust you to be a good boy?'

'Of course,' says John.

See John hop and skip over to where the display is being set up.

'Hello John,' says Mrs Havard.

'Hello Mrs Havard,' says John. What fun!

John says, 'That looks like an interesting display you are setting up there.'

Mrs Havard says, 'Yes, we've nearly finished now. I just have to set up the last of the fireworks on the top of this frame and we're done.'

John says, 'Can I help at all?' Kind John.

Mrs Havard says, 'As long as you are very careful and put on some gloves.'

See John put on some gloves and start unpacking and handing the fireworks to Mrs Havard.

John says, 'What will the display look like tonight?'

Mrs Havard says, 'If you are a good boy we will have lots of rockets and Catherine wheels and some mortar shells that will create a rising wave of colour behind the cricket pavilion. This racking contains the static lancework display, which when it's lit will spell out the name "Uckfield".'

Can you spell Uckfield?

See John hand fireworks to Mrs Havard.

Mrs Havard says, 'Nearly finished. If you could hand me up that three-sided firework in the box marked "Bermuda" to go on the top, we will be done.'

Soon, the display is ready. See John wave goodbye to Mrs Havard and hop and skip back to meet Janet by the toffee-apple stall.

Janet says, 'Who was that woman I saw you talking to?'

See the warning signs.

John says, 'That was Mrs Havard. She said she was going to put on a really impressive display for me later. She said that if I was a good boy, she'd create a rising effect behind the cricket pavilion, so I was only too happy to help cover her rack with lancework and hand up her Bermuda triangle.'

See Janet tip molten toffee down John's tights.

Hear the screams.

Poor John.

Janet and John Decorate the Church

Today, Janet and John are going to help put up the Christmas decorations at the local church.

Do you like Christmas decorations? John does.

Janet says, 'Will you stop getting glitter all over the carpet and hurry up John?'

See John finish putting sparkles in his beard and hair.

Janet says, 'It's quite cold this evening, so wrap up warm.'

John puts on his red fun-fur suit and thigh-

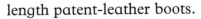

length patent-leather boots.

John is a popinjay.

See Janet and John walk down the lane to the church.

When they arrive at the church, there are lots of people already there.

Janet says, 'I'm going to see Pastor Kidneys about the programme of services for Christmas. Try to make yourself useful and see if you can behave for a change.'

'I will,' says John.

John is looking around to see what he can do when he sees Mrs Allen from the supermarket.

Mrs Allen is from East London. See the pie and mash.

'Hello Mrs Allen,' says John.

'Hello John,' says Mrs Allen. What fun!

Mrs Allen says, 'Perhaps you could help me decorate the tree in the vestry? We got a noble fir this year. It's quite an unusual tree.'

'Of course,' says John.

See John help Mrs Allen put baubles, lights and tinsel on the tree. See how it shines and sparkles.

Mrs Allen says, 'Can you give me a hand to sweep up the needles and glitter from the carpet?'

'Of course,' says John.

When the carpet is nice and clean, Mrs Allen says, 'All we have to do now is put the Christmas candles up on the organ and we're done. I always put away the decorations for the organ in this big box and mark it specially so no one touches it. I really look forward to this job, it means Christmas is nearly here.'

See John carry the big box over to the organ. See how strong John is.

Mrs Allen says, 'There is quite a lot of candle grease in the holders. We'll need to clean that out and get the drips off before we can put the new ones in. I've found that a warm spoon is the best thing to use.'

See John hop and skip to the kitchen to fetch a spoon.

See Mrs Allen heat the spoon up and scrape all of the old wax out of the holders and put new candles in.

Clever Mrs Allen.

Soon the decorations are finished and the candles lit. John waves goodbye to Mrs Allen and hops and skips off to meet Janet.

Janet is helping Pastor Kidneys clean out the incense burners.

'Hello Janet,' says John.

Janet says, 'Did you behave?'

'Yes,' says John. 'Mrs Allen asked if I would like to go into the vestry and help to trim her fir. After we'd got all the bits out of the carpet, she offered to help with the organ. She said that no one had been near her box since last Christmas, and we might need a warm spoon. She really looks forward to when she gets the big candles up and wax off the old organ.'

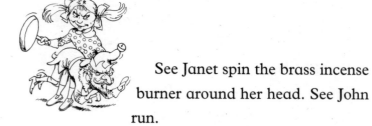

See Janet spin the brass incense burner around her head. See John run.

Run, John, run.

John Has a Sick Note

Today, John has decided to stay at home to play in the snow.

Do you like making snowmen? John does.

John's snowmen are all popinjays. See the bright sparkly clothes.

John was supposed to go to work, but John still has a sick note from the doctor because he has a broken fingernail.

Poor John.

John's friend Alan from Wealdstone, who has a part-time job as a bingo caller, has agreed to cover the ten minutes' work that John normally does.

Kind Alan.

Alan gets up early and gets the train into work. Alan does not have time for breakfast as it takes a long time to get from Wealdstone because of the snow.

When Alan arrives in London, he goes to the local delicatessen to pick up his breakfast.

'Ding-a-ling' goes the shop bell.

Alan sees Mrs Scott behind the counter.

Mrs Scott says, 'Hello Mr Dedicoat. Are you still having to cover for the old fellow who looks like Mr Pastry?'

'Yes,' says Alan.

Mrs Scott says, 'Normally, he comes in for his Wiener schnitzel and coffee for breakfast every day. He said that he needs the coffee to wake him up on the early shift. He used to really like these candied brandy snaps over here too.'

Alan says, 'I didn't know he had breakfast here.'

Mrs Scott says, 'When I first suggested the

schnitzel, he wasn't too keen to start with. I know that his wife doesn't like him having fried food, but now he loves them. Tell him that when he's better, the next time he comes in, I'll give him a pound off of his order.'

Kind Mrs Scott.

See Alan order the full cooked breakfast, fourteen rounds of toast and a big pot of coffee. Hungry Alan.

When Alan has finished his breakfast, he orders some cakes for his elevenses, then goes off to work.

When it is time to go home, Alan calls John on the telephone.

'Ring-ring' goes the phone.

Janet is making some sausage rolls in the kitchen. John likes sausage rolls. See Janet wipe the flour off of her hands and answer the phone.

Hear Janet shout to John to come in and speak to Alan.

See John hop and skip gaily in from the garden,

take off his cerise duffle coat with lace trim on the cuffs and hood, his bright orange wellingtons and his sparkly blue mittens on a string.

When John has finished talking, Janet says, 'Did Alan want to know when you would be back at work?'

John says, 'No. Alan was telling me that he saw the lady who usually wakes me up when I stay up in London. She remembered my speciality because I used to be indifferent. She also showed him some of the candied snaps I like and said that she'd give me a special treat next time I'm in and let me have a pound off on her schnitzel.'

Do you know how to make your face go purple? Janet does.

See Janet pick up the marble rolling pin that John bought her for her birthday.

See John run.

Run, John, run.

John Is Still Off Sick

Today, John has had to take some time off from his junior traffic-boy job at the BBC as he had an accident at the hairdresser's when they cut off one of his biggest curls. John tried wrapping it in a packet of frozen peas, but the hospital couldn't do anything. Poor John.

John was supposed to be doing some training for some of the new regional newsreaders. John likes training, as he gets paid extra. John likes money.

John's friend Alan has agreed to stand in for him. Kind Alan. Alan is a bingo caller from

Wealdstone. See the bollards.

When Alan arrives for the training, there are lots of people waiting. Alan is asked to look after one of the ladies from Ireland. Alan introduces himself to Mrs James. Mrs James is from Termonfeckin. See the castles.

Alan says, 'That's an unusual badge Mrs James.'

Mrs James says, 'Please call me Toinette. It's a badge from the Irish Countrywomen's Association.'

Alan says, 'Have you done anything like this before?'

Mrs James says, 'Yes. I worked at the BBC a long time ago as a studio assistant.'

Alan says, 'But you haven't done any broadcasting before?'

Mrs James says, 'No, but I did work with quite a lot of the presenters. I remember that we all used to go to the pub around the back. Some of the presenters used to drink quite a lot, but I only ever

had a glass of Beaune usually.'

Do you enjoy a glass of wine? Alan does. Paint Alan's nose red.

Alan says, 'Some of the presenters used to have a drink in the studio before going on air too.'

Mrs James says, 'Yes, I would quite often join them for a drop of Scotch. I was always a cup-half-full type of person,' she laughs. 'I remember one spry old traffic assistant called John who used to dress like a French duke. I used to get a tickly throat and he used to let me have some of his special throat lozenges, they always seemed to be loose in his trouser pocket rather than in the tin. I didn't like the throat spray as I always managed to get it up my nose.'

What fun!

See Alan take Mrs James through to the studio and show her what to do. Are you good at training? Alan is.

After the training is over, Alan waves goodbye

to Mrs James and calls John to let him know how it went.

'Ring-ring' goes the phone.

See John hop and skip to the phone.

When John has finished talking to Alan, Janet says, 'Who was that on the phone?'

John says, 'That was Alan. He was telling me that one of the ladies who was in today remembered me from the last time she was there. He said she was a full half-cup woman, who used to rummage around in my trousers for something for her tickle. She didn't like the spray very much because it always went up her nose. I remembered her when Alan said that she used to enjoy a Beaune round the back, then often had a stiff Johnny Walker chaser upstairs before going on air.'

See Janet select a large umbrella from the stand in the hall.

See John run.

Run, John, run.

John Is Still Poorly

Today, John is still off sick from work. John has a hangnail and some nasty split ends.

Are you a good patient? John isn't. See John bang on the bedroom floor with his sparkly barley-twist cane.

John was supposed to go to the Traffic Department Christmas lunch at a carvery in London, but didn't feel well enough. Poor John.

John's friend Alan from Wealdstone has agreed to go in his place and tell him all about it afterwards. Alan likes going to restaurants. See the elasticated waist.

Alan has arrived early at the carvery and is having a pint of amaretto shandy at the bar. Hear Alan shout, 'Same again barman!'

Soon, the rest of the Traffic Department people arrive in their party clothes. See the jeans and sweatshirts.

Everyone sits down at the table and Alan orders some wine. Alan likes wine.

Mrs Nott, the owner's wife, comes out to take their order. Alan hands back his menu and says, 'I'll have all of the starters and all of the main courses except the lamb as I am on a diet.' Greedy Alan.

Mrs Nott says, 'Very good sir. Where is the dandified old gentleman with the pink beard who normally comes along? I know he's very old, I hope he's still with us.'

Alan says, 'Yes, but he's off sick at the moment.'

Mrs Nott says, 'That's a shame, he used to tell me all about the best places to buy shoes from, and last year he gave me and my husband some really useful advice about preparing a spit roast. We were hoping he'd be here as we'd got extra redcurrant jelly in specially.'

Do you like shoes? Mrs Nott does. Mrs Nott is from Brighton.

Soon the food arrives. Alan gets out some party games, hats, crackers and blindfolds. Everyone takes turns to play the game where you identify your colleague by the sound they make when they are chewing. What fun!

After everyone has finished eating, they leave Alan at the bar and go home.

Later that evening, Alan calls John to tell him all about the party.

'Ring-ring' goes the telephone.

Janet answers the phone and takes it upstairs on a silver tray to John with some fresh blue satin pyjamas with pink piping and tassels.

See John pick up the phone and talk to Alan.

When John has finished speaking, Janet says,

'Did they have a nice party?'

'Yes,' says John. 'They all went to a very nice place near the office. Mrs Nott was saying that it was a shame I couldn't make it as last year I gave her a hot tip in the kitchen and helped her and her husband with a spit roast. I told her that there is no substitute for having really good-quality meat on hand. While her husband watched, I showed her how to rub some oil in to guarantee something she'd be only too happy to get her teeth into and to take care when inserting the rod so that the meat is evenly distributed at both ends. Afterwards, some people like to remove the meat and cover everything with the juices before resting. She was very disappointed I wasn't there as she'd already got extra jelly in.'

See Janet pin John to the bed and put big dents in the silver tea tray.

Hear the screams.

Poor John.

John Goes Cheese Shopping

Today, John is going to do some shopping for Janet.

John likes to go shopping, but he always has to have a list as Janet says he is as sharp as a bag of wet mice. Funny Janet.

See John putting on his best shopping clothes – cork-heeled patent-leather shoes, pink silk stockings with green brocade knee breeches, a lilac frock coat and a hat with a big feather. John is a popinjay.

Janet says, 'I want you to get a loaf of white

bread from the baker and some cheese for sandwiches from the delicatessen. Here is the list, and some money. Don't take too long as I have my shot-putting lesson this afternoon and I don't want to be late again.'

See John hop and skip down the road to the village.

John picks up a loaf of bread from the baker's, then trots across the road to the delicatessen. 'Ding-a-ling' goes the shop bell.

'Hello John,' says Mrs Dashell.

'Hello Mrs Dashell,' says John. What fun!

Mrs Dashell says, 'What can I do for you today John?'

John says, 'I want to get some cheese for sandwiches please.'

Mrs Dashell says, 'Well, you've come to the right place John, we have lots of different cheeses. My husband is the real expert, but he's away on business. Do you know which one you like best?'

John does not know which cheese to buy. See John blub.

'There, there,' says Mrs Dashell. 'Come and sit down in the office and I will bring you some little pieces of cheese to taste, then you can tell me which one you like.' Kind Mrs Dashell.

See John try lots of different cheeses. Do you like cheese? John does.

'This Mimolette from Lille is very popular,' says Mrs Dashell. 'You might also like to try this sausage, John. It's a rough country hunter from France.'

Do you know how to pronounce words carefully? John does.

When John has tried lots of cheese, he buys some for lunch and skips all the way home.

When John arrives home, Janet is getting ready to make the sandwiches. Janet says, 'You were gone a long time.'

'Yes,' says John. 'After I picked up the bread, I

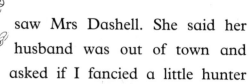

saw Mrs Dashell. She said her husband was out of town and asked if I fancied a little hunter sausage round the back. I had a big mouthful of her Mimolette, and she said that if I wanted to pop back for more at any time, I would be more than welcome.'

See Janet pick up the bread knife.

See John run.

Run, John, run.

Janet and John
Go to the Seaside

Today, it is a lovely day and Janet and John are going to the seaside.

John likes going to the seaside and is very excited. See the puddles.

Janet says, 'Hurry up John, we want to make sure we get a good parking space.'

See John putting his pink sparkly swimming costume and orange swimming hat with purple flowers in his bag, and getting out his fishing net and bucket and spade.

Soon Janet straps John into the safety seat and

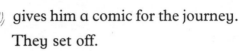

gives him a comic for the journey.

They set off.

When Janet and John arrive at the seaside, Janet parks the car near the fishing jetty.

Janet says, 'I'm going to walk into town to get some lunch. You stay here and play, and don't get into mischief.'

'I won't,' says John.

See John hop and skip along to the fishing jetty to look at the boats.

Do you like boats? John does.

John sees Mrs Billingsley. Mrs Billingsley is helping Mrs Hutchings to lift the fishing nets on to the boat. They are very tired and are out of breath.

John says, 'Can I help you ladies?'

Kind John.

Mrs Hutchings says, 'Yes please John. We've just had a quick run around the bay and need to see what we've caught. If you could help us to get the net near to the surface, we can get the winch on it then and bring it on to the dock.'

See John pulling on the net. See how strong John is.

Mrs Billingsley says, 'Thank you very much John.'

John says, 'What sort of fish do you catch?'

Mrs Hutchings says, 'Normally, we get a few flatfish, the odd crab and mackerel, but we don't go out very far.'

John says, 'I go sailing in my boat, but I mostly go round and round in the harbour.'

Mrs Billingsley says, 'Could you take a photo of both of us by the side of the boat? It's for a special tourism magazine advert.'

'Yes, of course,' says John. John knows all about cameras. John used to work a camera for the BBC. Clever John.

When John has taken the photograph, he walks back to the car park to meet Janet.

Soon, Janet arrives back with a big carrier bag

 full of food.

Janet says, 'Have you been a good boy John?'

'Yes,' says John. 'I saw Mrs Billingsley and Mrs Hutchings. They told me between their pants that they were looking for a big strong man, so I helped them pull up their fishnets to just below sea level, then took some photographs for a special magazine.'

Do you know what a ferocious uppercut is?

Janet does.

So does John.

Poor John.

John Goes to the Printer's

Today, John is going to run some errands in the village. John likes to run errands as it means he can get out his purple sparkly bicycle with training wheels.

See John put on his special cycling clothes – a yellow and orange striped Lycra bodysuit with orange boots, a shiny purple helmet and matching cape. John is a popinjay.

Janet says, 'On the way to the post office, you can drop the details of the poster for the bring-and-buy sale in at the printer's for me. While you are gone, I'll be turning the compost bin.'

See John put the post and the envelope Janet has given him for the printer in his shiny black handbag and whizz down the road.

When John arrives at the printer's, he notices that his front tyre is rather flat. John does not have his pump with him. Silly John. See John blub.

John sees Mrs Dickins. Mrs Dickins says, 'What's the matter John?'

John says, 'I have a flat tyre and I need to get to the post box.'

Mrs Dickins says, 'Never mind, I have to go to the post box soon so I will take you in my car. While we are gone, I will ask one of the boys to pump it up for you with the air line. Do you have the envelope with the details for the poster John?'

'Yes,' says John, and hands over the envelope.

John says, 'It must be very interesting working at the printer's.'

Mrs Dickins says, 'Yes, it is. Most of the time we are quite busy and it is my responsibility to pass the jobs to be done to the printers and designers I work with, but I also have to make sure that the post goes out on time. Quite a lot of the post has to go to France, but there is none today so I don't need to go all the way to the post office.'

See Mrs Dickins put the post in a bag and take John down to her car.

Soon they are at the post box and John can post his letters.

Mrs Dickins takes John back to the printer's and, sure enough, his flat tyre has some air in it and John can go home.

John thanks Mrs Dickins and cycles home with his cape flapping in the wind behind him.

When John gets home, Janet is in the garden emptying the compost bin. Janet says, 'You were gone a long time John.'

'Yes,' says John. 'When I got to the printer's I noticed that I needed a pump. Mrs Dickins said she'd be happy to help out. She said it was her responsibility to give the printers their instructions and hand jobs out in the office, so she was just the right person.

'She was fairly certain that she didn't have any French letters, so she didn't go all the way, but was always keen to get her mail off quickly, so she took me in her car, then afterwards brought me back to the office, by which time my chopper was ready to go again.'

See Janet push John into the compost bin and put the lid on.

Poor John.

John Goes to an Employment Agency

Today, John has an interview at an employment agency.

Janet says that as John only works one day a week, like his friend Terry, he is starting to annoy her.

Do you know how to give helpful advice on household chores and shopping?

John puts on his smartest interview clothes – a bright green morning suit with pink piping and a top hat, a bright orange frilly shirt with a matching bow tie and silver shoes with black spats.

Janet says, 'I thought it was an employment

agency, not an audition for Fop Idol.' Funny Janet.

Janet says, 'Don't forget to pick up something for your lunch as I will be at my flower-arranging class – and not just sweets and crisps either.'

See John wave goodbye to Janet as he hops and skips gaily down the road to the bus stop.

When John arrives in town he goes to the sweetshop and buys lots of sweets and a big bag of orange cheesy snacks from Mrs Slade. Naughty John!

Soon it is time for John's appointment. John is still eating his cheesy snacks when he rings the bell at the office door, 'ding-a-ling'.

Mrs Whitehead answers the door and takes John through reception to her office.

Mrs Whitehead says, 'I need you to fill in this application form, then we will see what we have on the books that might suit you. We don't get much call for circus ringmasters so you might

need to wear some more sensible clothes. As you seem to have brought your lunch with you, you could at least offer me some.'

See John give the last of the snacks to Mrs Whitehead. Kind John.

Mrs Whitehead says, 'Well, you've passed the first test John, if I don't like the look of someone I don't let them get any further than reception, although your dress sense made me think about blowing you out right away.'

See John doing his best joined-up handwriting on the application form. When John has finished there are only a few smudges and some orange crumbs on the form that have fallen out of John's beard.

Mrs Whitehead says, 'What sort of work are you looking for John?'

John says, 'I'd like to be a judge or a mayor please as they have lovely clothes.'

Mrs Whitehead says, 'We don't have any vacancies for either of those right now, but there are a couple of jobs that might suit you. I'll submit your application tomorrow. If you'd like to pop back next week, I'll let you know how I got on and will give you some hints about overcoming ageism.'

'Thank you,' says John.

See John wave goodbye to Mrs Whitehead and hop and skip back to the bus station.

When John gets home, Janet is making a floral arrangement with some gladioli.

Janet says, 'Do you have a job yet?'

John says, 'Not yet, but I saw Mrs Whitehead. She said that she would show me how I can get on, as at my age it can be a bit difficult. She said that she had thought about blowing me out in reception, but after I'd let her have a handful of my Wotsits, she said that there were a couple of positions on her desk that she'd like to try.'

Do you know what a face like thunder looks like?

John does. See John run.

Run, John, run.

Janet and John Go to the Park

Today, the sun is shining and Janet and John are going to the park. Janet wants to look at the new flowerbeds with all of the lovely spring flowers.

John likes going to the park. See John put on his bright orange dungarees, a blue and white striped jumper, pink ankle boots and a yellow scarf. John is a dandy.

Janet says, 'If you are a good boy, you can go on the swings while I'm looking at the flowers.'

Do you like swinging? John does.

When Janet and John arrive at the park, Janet

says, 'I'll see you back at the park entrance in an hour. Don't be late!'

'I won't,' says John, and skips merrily down the path to the playground, but the swings have a 'wet paint' notice on them. See John blub.

While John is wiping away his tears, he sees Mrs Grace waving at him from over the hedge.

'Hello John,' says Mrs Grace. 'Can you help me? We are playing bowls and one of them has gone under the hedge. It's a white one. I can't see it from here. Could you look for me please?'

'Of course,' says John.

Soon John sees the small white ball in the ditch and returns it to Mrs Grace.

Mrs Grace says, 'Thank you John. Have you ever played bowls?'

See John shake his head.

Mrs Grace says, 'Would you like to try?'

'Yes please,' says John, and hops and skips round the path to the gate.

Mrs Grace says, 'The idea is to bowl this small white ball called the jack or kitty down the rink, which is the strip of grass we're standing on now. Then we take turns to see how close to that we can get with the larger bowls. When you have a group of bowls all around the jack it is called the "head".'

Mrs Grace rolls the jack down the green then shows John how to hold the bowls. See John's first attempt hit the jack hard and roll it behind the clubhouse.

Mrs Grace says, 'That jack would now be out of bounds and would be what is called a "dead end". That tactic is sometimes useful when your opposition is winning the match. But for normal play, that was a bit hard, so let's try it again a little slower.'

See John roll the bowl down the green. Mrs Grace says, 'Bravo John, that was nice and smooth with a really good roll of your wrist and release. You even managed to get the curve right so that your bowl was close to the jack.'

See John blush.

John plays several more games and gets better and better. Clever John.

Soon it is time for John to meet Janet, so he waves goodbye to Mrs Grace and hops and skips back to meet Janet.

Soon Janet arrives at the park entrance. Janet says, 'Did you behave John?'

'Yes,' says John. 'Mrs Grace called me over and wanted me to get on my hands and knees to see if I could see her kitty under the hedge. She invited me into the club to join her for some games. My first attempt was a bit hard for her and I had a dead end and a jack off behind the clubhouse. Mrs Grace showed me a couple of pointers and said she really liked my smooth wrist action and fluid release and said I could come back at any time.'

Do you know how to deliver a powerful uppercut?

Janet does.

See John sitting on the ground
looking at all the pretty stars.

Poor John.

Janet and John Go to a Folk-music Festival

Today, it has stopped raining for a whole morning so Janet and John are going to a folk-music festival.

Do you like folk music?

See John put on his best court-jester's outfit with pointy shoes and a hat with bells. John is a fop.

Janet says, 'Hurry up John, the music starts in an hour and you haven't even put your make-up on yet.'

See John pluck his eyebrows and put on some fake tan and sparkly lip gloss.

Soon, Janet has strapped John into his booster seat and they set off in the car.

When they arrive, Janet parks the car and they make their way to the entrance to the festival.

There are lots of people there already – see the cheesecloth.

Janet pays their entrance fees and they walk around some of the stalls selling free-range joss sticks and organic face paint.

Janet says, 'As we were so late starting out, I'm going off to get us some lunch. I'll see you over by the morris dancers in half an hour. Try to behave!'

'I will,' says John.

See John hop and skip gaily along the rows of stalls and displays swinging his shiny gold handbag.

John stops by a display of musical instruments.

There are lots of people playing music on the display. See John dance.

Mrs Coker, who is playing the fiddle, says,

'That's very nice dancing. You should be in one of the morris sides. Do you play a musical instrument too?'

John says, 'I play the church organ.'

Mrs Coker says, 'That's probably a bit big to bring with you.'

Funny Mrs Coker.

John says, 'How many instruments do you play?'

Mrs Coker says, 'I used to play the Kerry whistle, but it was quite difficult to master as the hole for the bottom note was quite difficult to reach, but the latest ones have had it repositioned for easier access. I play the fiddle now and have just recently started to learn the dulcimer. It used to be considered a woman's instrument, but everyone plays it now.'

See Mrs Coker show John how to play the dulcimer.

Clever Mrs Coker.

Soon it is time for John to go back to meet Janet. See John wave goodbye to Mrs Coker and hop and skip over to the morris-dancing display.

Soon Janet arrives with some lunch. Janet says, 'Did you behave John?'

'Yes,' says John. 'I saw Mrs Coker, who was very friendly. She said that my organ was probably a bit big to manage today. She said she preferred a fiddle and took up the dulcimer after that. She was very happy to show me what to do.'

See Janet borrow a big stick from one of the morris men. See John run.

Run, John, run.

John Goes to the
Department Store

Today, Janet and John are going shopping.

Shopping is one of John's favourite things apart from redcurrant jelly.

John is very excited and Janet has to change his pull-ups three times.

John puts on his best shopping clothes – a purple velvet suit with flared trousers, a yellow silk shirt with pink flowers on it, a blue silk cravat and a big floppy lime-green hat with an ostrich feather in it. John is a dandy.

See Janet and John walk down the lane to the bus

stop. Janet has to put on John's reins to stop him running up and down the stairs on the bus, licking the windows and ringing the bell. Naughty John.

When they arrive in town, Janet says, 'I'm going to the post office and then to the butcher's to pick up some mince for dinner.'

Sometimes Janet makes her own mince and lets John help. John is very good at mincing.

Janet says, 'You can go to the shops on your own if you promise to behave.'

'I will,' says John.

Janet says, 'I'll see you back at the bus stop in half an hour.'

See John wave goodbye to Janet and hop and skip down the road, swinging his sparkly shoulder bag.

John goes into the department store to look at clothes. John likes looking at clothes.

John is walking through the ladies' section when he sees Mrs Brindley. Mrs Brindley is from

Southend. See the white stilettos.

'Hello John,' says Mrs Brindley.

'Hello Mrs Brindley,' says John.

What fun!

Mrs Brindley says, 'Are you looking for anything in particular today John?'

John says, 'Not especially, the men's clothes in here are a bit plain. I like sparkly, colourful clothes.'

Mrs Brindley says, 'The only clothes we have like that in here are in the ladies' foundation garments. I look after that section, but I don't think there would be anything in there that would suit you.' Funny Mrs Brindley.

Mrs Brindley says, 'Perhaps you could buy some nice things for Janet? It's quite quiet today, so I could take some time to pick out something really nice.'

John says, 'Do they cost a lot of money? I only work as a part-time announcer now so I don't have very much to spend.'

Mrs Brindley says, 'Some of the silks, satins

and lace things are quite expensive, but you could buy her something for a special occasion. This silk slip is just in this week and is very good value at only fifty pounds.'

See John go pale and clutch his purse. John says, 'That's much more than I can afford. Perhaps I could save up and come back another time.'

Mrs Brindley says, 'That's alright John, we'll be having a sale in two weeks and the prices will go down. When you come back, ask for me at the help desk and I will make sure you get exactly the right thing.'

See John wave goodbye to Mrs Brindley and skip off gaily down the road. John buys some comics and sweets and stands outside a furniture shop that sells mirrors, admiring his reflection.

Soon it is time to meet Janet. John wipes the liquorice from his beard and finishes his sherbet fountain on the way back to the bus stop. John

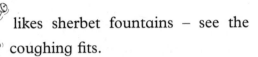

likes sherbet fountains – see the coughing fits.

When Janet arrives, she has two big bags of groceries.

Janet says, 'Did you behave?'

'Yes,' says John. 'I went into the department store and saw Mrs Brindley. I found her under clothes on the floor of the ladies' section and she asked me if there was anything special I would like, and suggested that I might like to splash out on her new underwear. She told me it would only cost fifty pounds and said it was quite quiet today so I could take as much time as I wanted. When I said that I couldn't afford her prices, she said to come back in two weeks and ask to look up Mrs Brindley on the front desk and she would definitely drop them for me.'

Can you make your knuckles go white? Janet can.

See Janet rub mince into John's hair.

Poor John.

Janet and John Go to a Spring Fair

Today, Janet and John are going to a spring fair at the vicarage.

John puts on some nice seasonal clothes – a daffodil-yellow tailcoat with bright green trousers, a frilly white shirt and purple patent-leather cowboy boots. John is a popinjay.

Janet says, 'Hurry up John or we'll be late for the opening ceremony.'

John quickly finishes his make-up, takes out the heated rollers from his beard and puts on some cologne.

See Janet and John walk down the lane to the vicarage.

When they arrive, Pastor Kidneys welcomes them and says to Janet, 'I have the metal skewers you loaned me for the barbecue last week. If you'd like to come around to the kitchen, I'll let you have them.'

Janet says to John, 'I won't be long, try not to get into trouble.'

'I won't,' says John.

See John walk around some of the spring displays.

John sees Mrs Bickerdyke.

'Eh-up Fluffywhiskers,' says Mrs Bickerdyke. Mrs Bickerdyke is from Yorkshire – see the puddings. Mrs Bickerdyke says, 'Aren't the spring flowers wonderful this year John?'

Do you like flowers? John does.

Mrs Bickerdyke says, 'If you have five minutes John, you should go and see Mrs Gregory's obedience classes on the back lawn.'

Do you know what obedience classes are?

Janet thinks John should go to obedience classes as she has a lot of trouble getting him to wash behind his ears.

See John hop and skip around to the back garden.

Mrs Gregory is showing everyone how her giant schnauzer, Popsie, can fetch lots of different items on command.

When the display is finished, John says to Mrs Gregory, 'That was very good. Did it take a long time to train your dog?'

Mrs Gregory says, 'It took about six months. But this latest trick is the most impressive one of all, as Popsie can pick up six ping-pong balls at the same time without breaking or denting any of them. We have a special charity event on Saturday. I normally run the bingo, but as it's an animal welfare event my husband said it would be a good idea if Popsie were to pick the balls and bring them

to me rather than using the machine. It will give me a chance to put my feet up for a change.'

John says, 'Yes, that would be fun.'

John waves goodbye to Mrs Gregory as he sees Janet coming down the garden path.

Janet says, 'Who was that woman I saw you talking to?'

See the warning signs.

John says, 'That was Mrs Gregory. She showed me some of the tricks she's been learning with her Popsie. She can pick up six ping-pong balls at a time and on Saturday her husband has said that as it's a special fundraising event she can put her feet up for a change and replace the bingo machine with her giant schnauzer.'

See Janet go purple.

See Janet chase John down the garden path with a big bunch of skewers.

See John run.

Run, John, run.

Janet and John Go into Town

Today, Janet and John are going shopping in Uckfield. John likes shopping.

Janet says, 'Hurry up John or we'll miss the bus and have to wait another half-hour.'

John says, 'I'm just waiting for my beard straighteners to warm up.'

John is a popinjay.

Janet says, 'If you're not ready in one minute, there will be no redcurrant jelly for you for a month.'

Do you like redcurrant jelly? John does.

Janet puts on John's reins to stop him skipping

all the way to the bus stop.

When they arrive in Uckfield, Janet says, 'You can either come with me to the shops to get a new bicycle lock, and the library, or you can look around the shops on your own – as long as you promise that you will behave!'

'I will,' says John.

Janet says, 'I'll see you back at the bus stop in an hour.'

See John wave goodbye to Janet and hop and skip gaily down the high street.

There are lots of shops in the high street, but not very many that sell bright clothes, toys or sweets, so John looks at the windows of some of the other shops.

While John is looking at the shops, he sees Mrs Bickerdyke.

'Eh-up Fluffywhiskers,' says Mrs Bickerdyke. Mrs Bickerdyke is from Yorkshire – see the dark satanic mills.

Mrs Bickerdyke says, 'If you've nowt on, Mrs

Fletcher in the estate agent's could do with a hand. She's got two out sick and the shop is full of people.'

John says, 'I am only window-shopping anyway, so I would be happy to help.' Kind John.

John waves goodbye to Mrs Bickerdyke and skips over to the estate agent's.

'Ding-a-ling' goes the door.

There are lots of people queuing to see Mrs Fletcher and the phone is ringing.

John says to Mrs Fletcher, 'Mrs Bickerdyke said you could do with a hand, so I've come to help.'

'Thank you,' says Mrs Fletcher.

See John answer the phone and take down some messages, then make Mrs Fletcher a cup of tea.

Soon, all of the people have gone and Mrs Fletcher is able to have a little rest.

John says, 'Is there anything else I can do?'

Mrs Fletcher says, 'You could put up these house details in the window, it's a bit of a stretch for me.'

'Of course,' says John. See how tall John is.

While John is pinning up the house details on the board in the window, he sees Melanie Frontage outside.

Melanie Frontage has a shop with black windows and sells special things for married people.

Melanie Frontage comes into the shop.

'Hello Johnny,' says Melanie Frontage. 'I didn't know you worked here.'

John says, 'I'm just helping out as Mrs Fletcher is very busy.'

Melanie Frontage says, 'I'd like some more information about that house you have just put in the window. It looks suitable for my niece, but it might be a bit small. Perhaps she could see if it could have an extension?'

John says, 'Yes, the semi-detached one. I will have Mrs Fletcher speak to you about it.'

Soon it is time for John to meet Janet.

Mrs Fletcher gives John ten pounds for helping her out.

See John skip back down the road to the bus stop swinging his sparkly handbag.

When Janet arrives, John says, 'Hello Janet.'

Janet says, 'Have you been a good boy?'

'Yes,' says John. 'I saw Mrs Bickerdyke. She told me that if I was interested, and had nothing on, Mrs Fletcher was a bit desperate, so I popped along to help her out. I had to wait for the queue to die down before I could get her to put her feet up for ten minutes. She was ever so grateful and gave me ten pounds. Then I saw Melanie Frontage. She could see I had a nice semi on in the window and was very interested in seeing if it could be extended.'

See Janet get out her new D-ring bicycle lock.

See Janet lock John's neck to the bus stop and storm off down the road.

Poor John.

Janet and John Go to a Collectors' Fair

Today, Janet and John are going to a collectors' fair.

Do you know what a collectors' fair is?

Janet says that a collectors' fair is a place where you pay good money for more old rubbish to put in the shed.

John likes putting things in his shed.

Janet says, 'Hurry up John, otherwise you'll miss all the bargains.'

See John put on a red velvet suit with zebra-striped trim, a feather boa and a big floppy hat.

John is a popinjay.

See John hop and skip gaily down the road to the bus stop.

When Janet and John arrive at the collectors' fair, there are lots of stalls selling all sorts of things – stamps, coins, silver, porcelain and books.

Janet says, 'I'm going to look for some brasses for the fireplace. Have a look around the stalls and don't get into trouble.'

'I won't,' says John

John sees a stall selling old comics. John likes comics.

Mrs Hill, who is running the stall, says, 'Hello John. Are you looking for anything in particular?'

John says, 'I'm just looking at all of these lovely comics. They remind me of when I was young. I have a lot of comics at home in my shed.'

Mrs Hill says, 'Some of these are becoming very collectible now. The first edition of the *Valiant* makes over a hundred pounds, as long as you still have the elastic band-powered rocket that came with it.'

John says, 'Do you know, I think I might have that. They did lots of free gifts. I remember a card with brown paper in a triangular shape which, when swung with your arm, flapped out making a bang like a paper bag bursting. I mostly have *The Beano*, *The Whizzer* and *The Victor*. I like "Gorgeous Gus" in *The Victor* because he is always dressed very nicely.'

Mrs Hill says, 'I'd be very interested to see if you have the first edition of *The Whizzer* but I would have thought that you were more likely to enjoy *The Dandy*.'

See John blush. Paint John's face red.

While John is talking to Mrs Hill, he sees Mrs Bickerdyke.

'Eh-up Fluffywhiskers,' says Mrs Bickerdyke.

Mrs Bickerdyke is from Yorkshire. See Nora Batty.

Mrs Bickerdyke says, 'I didn't know you collected comics John. I have hundreds at home.

When I was a girl, I used to keep a big stack of them outside the "smallest room". The number of times I stood there in a tizzy because I couldn't decide whether I wanted a *Twinkle* or a *Bunty*.'

Do you sometimes have trouble deciding whether you want a *Twinkle* or a *Bunty*?

John says, 'I think I have an early copy of *Twinkle* at home that was in my shed when I moved to my house. Would you like it?'

'That'd be grand,' says Mrs Bickerdyke. 'I'll be happy to pay you, or I could swap you for some *Beanos*. I do like those "Little Plum" comic strips.'

John says, 'I have lots of those. You must come around for a read. You can have the *Twinkle* on me.'

Kind John.

John sees Janet. Janet has bought a pair of brass coal tongs and a poker. John hops and skips over to meet her. What fun!

Janet says, 'Who were those women you were

talking to?'

John says, 'I was talking to Mrs Hill about when we were young. Mrs Hill said that she'd like to see my old *Whizzer* and if I still had the pocket-rocket that she first saw in 1963, she'd be happy to give me a hundred pounds. Then Mrs Bickerdyke said she'd like to have a look at my "Little Plums".'

See Janet clamp John's trousers with the coal tongs and chase him down the road with the poker.

See John run.

Run, John, run.

John is in the Garden

Today is a lovely sunny day. Janet is going to her cage-fighting class at the village hall.

Janet says, 'I'm just going out now John. Don't forget that Mrs Langley is coming over to drop off some curtain samples later.'

'I won't,' says John.

Janet says, 'While I'm out, why don't you tidy up your dressing table? It's full of old perfume bottles and make-up tubes.'

See John wave goodbye to Janet as she drives off down the lane.

As soon as Janet has gone, John starts to tidy

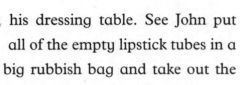 his dressing table. See John put all of the empty lipstick tubes in a big rubbish bag and take out the old nail-varnish bottles to the recycling bin.

John sees a big snail on the top of the recycling bin and uses some of his old nail varnish to give it a makeover. See the pretty sparkly pink, blue and gold snail.

Just as John is about to put on a coat of clear varnish and some crystals, he hears the front doorbell.

'Ding-dong'.

See John hop and skip in from the garden and open the door.

'Hello John,' says Mrs Langley.

'Hello Mrs Langley,' says John.

What fun!

Mrs Langley says, 'Is Janet in?'

'No,' says John. 'But she said that I could take the fabric samples for her.'

Mrs Langley says, 'While I'm here, I may as

well have a look at the windows so that I can be sure of how much fabric to quote for.'

See John take Mrs Langley through to the sitting room.

Mrs Langley gets out a big tape measure and writes down some of the measurements on an order book.

Mrs Langley says, 'Could you give me a hand please John? I can manage the drop of the curtains, but not the width. If you could hold one end of the tape for me it would be a great help.'

See John help Mrs Langley to measure the windows. Kind John.

Mrs Langley says, 'I see that you have an eye for colour John, what do you think of this chenille?'

John says, 'I like that one very much. I have a suit that is nearly the same colour blue.'

John is a fop.

Mrs Langley says, 'Chenille is very good for privacy as it's quite thick material. In the kitchen, you should probably have something light and washable like a cotton, or seersucker. I will leave some samples in a similar blue, and an estimate.'

See Mrs Langley write down the prices and leave some sample fabrics for Janet.

When Janet gets home, John is back in the garden, varnishing snails.

Janet says, 'Did you tidy your dressing table?'

'Yes,' says John. 'Mrs Langley came round and recommended chenille in the sitting room as it would look better if the neighbours couldn't see in. She managed the length all right, but the width was a bit much for her as she wasn't able to stretch that far, then she asked if I would prefer a little blue seersucker in the kitchen as it would be easier to wash.'

See Janet boil.

Do you know how to perform a close-quarter elbow strike? Janet does.

Poor John.

John Goes to a Wine Tasting

Today, John has finished work early. John has a part-time job at the BBC. John only does about twenty minutes of work a week, but no one seems to mind him coming in.

John collects his handbag and his floppy hat with a feather from his desk and goes to catch the train home.

On the way to the train station, John sees a sign outside a wine shop that says, 'Free wine tasting today'.

Do you like free things? John does.

John is only allowed to have a few glasses of wine, otherwise he goes all floppy.

John is looking at all of the people trying glasses of wine. John is very thirsty.

John sees a lady on one of the stalls with a big tray of glasses of red wine.

See John skip gaily over to the stall.

The lady has a badge on that says, 'Mrs Gregory'.

'Hello Mrs Gregory,' says John. 'My name is John and I work for the BBC.'

Mrs Gregory says, 'In that case, would you like to try something a bit special? I have a delightful wine from Nice called a Bellet that you can't normally find here.'

'Yes please,' says John.

Mrs Gregory says, 'I expect it to be snapped up by the London merchants as soon as they see it.'

See John drink a big glass of wine.

Mrs Gregory says, 'Try this one. This is called

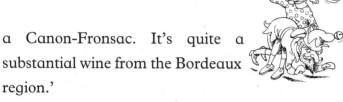

a Canon-Fronsac. It's quite a substantial wine from the Bordeaux region.'

John drinks two glasses and starts to go a bit wobbly.

Mrs Gregory says, 'As I'm rather busy, perhaps you wouldn't mind handing around some more wine for me?'

'Not at all,' says John.

Mrs Gregory says, 'This one is called a Semillon. It's a sweet white wine from Bordeaux and a firm favourite with our clients.'

See John put lots of glasses of the wine on a tray and wave his feathery hat at passers-by.

John stops a lady with a badge on that says, 'Mrs Middler'.

'Hello Mrs Middler,' says John.

Mrs Middler says, 'I like your purple velvet suit. Do you have any Beaune?'

John says, 'No, I don't, but I do have this lovely wine from Bordeaux if you'd like to give it a try.'

See Mrs Middler take a glass of wine and taste it.

Mrs Middler says, 'Most of the wine merchants don't swallow the wine, but with wine this good, I always do.'

Soon it is time for John to catch his train. See John wave goodbye to all of his friends and walk carefully down the road to the station.

When John arrives home, Janet is doing the ironing.

'Hello Janet,' says John.

Janet says, 'You are very late this evening.'

See the warning signs.

John says, 'I went along to a party on the way home. I saw Mrs Gregory. She was expecting some of the London merchants to jump on her Bellet, and told me I could have a try. Then she let me sample her Canon-Fronsacs. After that, I saw Mrs Middler. She was after a decent Beaune. But as soon as she saw I had a Semillon, she just had to have a mouthful. She said that lots of people spit it out, but she never does.'

See Janet tie John to the ironing board and turn the iron setting to steam.

Hear the screams.

Poor John.

Janet and John Go to a Craft Fair

Today, Janet and John are going to a craft fair.

John wants to buy some handmade lace. John has lace on the edges of nearly all his clothes. John is a fop.

Janet says, 'Hurry up John, otherwise we won't miss the traffic.'

John says, 'I'm nearly finished with my beard straighteners and I should really give my toenails another coat of varnish.'

See Janet do a cross face.

Janet is good at cross faces.

Soon, John is strapped into his safety seat in the back of the car and they set off.

When they arrive, Janet parks the car and puts on John's reins to make sure he doesn't get into mischief.

Janet sees Pastor Kidneys by the refreshment stall.

Janet says, 'I need to talk to Pastor Kidneys about the bring-and-buy sale. If I take your reins off, do you think you can keep out of trouble?'

John says, 'Of course.'

Janet says, 'I'll see you back here in half an hour. Do try to behave!'

'I will,' says John.

See John looking at all of the displays. There are homemade cosmetics, cakes and sweets. John likes sweets. See the cavities.

John stops to look at a display of hand-spinning.

See John watch some ladies use a big spinning wheel to make wool.

John does not wear very much wool. All John's clothes are made of satin, silk and velvet.

Mrs Grayston, who is doing some of the spinning, asks if anyone would like to try spinning some wool. John says, 'Yes please.'

Mrs Grayston sits John down at the spinning wheel and shows him how to spin the raw wool into yarn. Clever Mrs Grayston.

John says, 'What kind of wool is this please?'

Mrs Grayston says, 'This wool is from some of my Clun-Forest sheep. They are very versatile as they can give milk and are good for meat too. The wool can be a little difficult to handle at first, so perhaps we should start you off with some wool from some of my Welsh mountain sheep.'

John says, 'It's making my hands very greasy.'

Mrs Grayston says, 'That's the lanolin in the wool. It keeps your hands wonderfully soft. Now that you have the hang of two-ply, let's see how you get on with four.'

See John working the spinning wheel.

Mrs Grayston says, 'Very good John. Let's see how you get on with the rougher wool from the Norfolk horn. They aren't used for spinning very much as the wool is quite coarse. You have to be careful how you handle it or you could just end up with felt.'

See John make three big balls of wool. Clever John.

Soon it is time for John to meet Janet.

See John hop and skip gaily back to the refreshment stall.

Janet is just buying some cheesecake.

Do you like cheesecake?

Janet says, 'Did you behave John?'

'Yes,' says John. 'Mrs Grayston was letting me handle the wool from her Clun Forest. She told me I was very good at four-ply but told me to be careful or I might get felt, then she let me try some Welsh mountain and gave me a hand with the

Norfolk horn, which was quite rough.'

Do you know how to make your whole head go purple? Janet does.

See Janet rub cheesecake into John's hair.

Poor John.

Janet and John
Go to a County Show

Today, Janet and John are going to a county show.

John puts on his purple tweed plus fours, a bright orange hacking jacket, yellow knee socks and a waxed cotton handbag.

John is a popinjay.

Janet says, 'Hurry up John, or we won't get a parking space.'

John says, 'I just need to wait for my nail varnish to dry, otherwise it will smudge.'

See Janet pull John's ear.

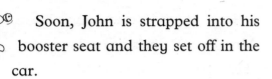

Soon, John is strapped into his booster seat and they set off in the car.

John likes going in the car, but he is not very often allowed to drive because he goes too fast.

When they arrive, Janet parks the car and puts on John's reins so he doesn't make a nuisance of himself.

See Janet looking at a stall selling antique fireplaces, coal buckets, pokers and brass companion sets. Janet says, 'While I'm shopping, why don't you go over and watch the displays in the main arena? I'll see you back here in half an hour – do try to behave!'

'I will,' says John, and hops and skips gaily over to the parade ring.

When John arrives at the parade ring, there are lots of people with horses.

John sees Mrs Frost. 'Hello Mrs Frost,' says John.

'Hello John,' says Mrs Frost. What fun!

John says, 'Is that your horse Mrs Frost? She's very big isn't she?'

Mrs Frost says, 'Yes, this is my Percheron mare. I've just finished clipping her and dressing her mane and tail ready for the parade. Percherons are a working breed and used to be used for ploughing.'

John says, 'Do you ride her at all?'

Mrs Frost says, 'Not very often. Because she's used to ploughing traces she doesn't respond very well to a riding bit. She's probably a bit too big for you to ride, especially in those tight trousers, but some of my friends are on the other side of the parade ring and have brought their hunters, which are used for riding all the time. If you'd like to come along I was just going over to see if they have finished getting the horses unloaded.'

'Yes please,' says John.

See John and Mrs Frost walk to the other side of the parade ring. Mrs Frost introduces John to her friends, Mrs Shelsher and Mrs Sutton.

Mrs Shelsher says, 'I have just tacked up my horse Topsy. He's a bit excitable today as I've just got him out of the horsebox, but if you want to, you can sit in the saddle.'

'Thank you Mrs Shelsher,' says John. 'That would be very nice.'

See Mrs Shelsher show John how to check that the saddle is on tight enough by adjusting the girth and which side of the horse to mount from.

Mrs Sutton shows John how to hold the reins and says, 'Don't hold them too tight. He has quite a soft mouth and even with a rubber-coated bit it will hurt him if you pull too hard.'

Mrs Shelsher says, 'You should always wear a hard hat John. What size do you take?'

John says, 'Seven and a quarter.'

Mrs Shelsher fetches John a hard hat from her horsebox and tries it on John's head. Mrs Sutton helps John to do up the chinstrap and pulls on the hat to make sure it is a good tight fit. Soon John is sitting in the saddle while Mrs Sutton walks Topsy around the parade ring. John is a little nervous. See the damp patch.

Soon it is time for John to meet Janet. See John wave goodbye to all his friends and hop and skip back to see Janet.

'Hello Janet,' says John.

Janet says, 'Did you behave?'

'Yes,' says John. 'I saw Mrs Frost, she had just finished clipping her Percheron and said that I could try mounting her. But she said that as she was rather large, I might have a little trouble getting my leg over in these tight trousers, but she took me to see some of her friends and said I could have much more fun with fourteen hands and a soft mouth. Mrs Shelsher let me try her Topsy. She gave my girth a good tug to make sure I wouldn't fall off and Mrs Sutton made sure I had some proper protection and let me have a rubber-

coated bit too.'

Can you put a ninety-degree bend in a two-foot brass poker?

Janet can.

Poor John.

John Has Fun with a Bike

Today, it is a bright sunny day and John is going for a ride on his scooter. John likes riding his scooter.

Janet says, 'Make sure you wrap up well John as it's not as warm as it looks.'

See John put on a one-piece pink cashmere catsuit with mother-of-pearl buttons and silver elbow patches, black furry ankle boots, a purple balaclava and matching scarf. John is a popinjay.

Janet says, 'Don't be late back as we have spaghetti and meatballs for lunch.'

John likes spaghetti and meatballs – see the sauce splashes on the ceiling.

John waves goodbye to Janet and scoots down the road as fast as he can, with his scarf flapping in the breeze.

When John gets to the village green, he stops outside the village shop to get his breath back. He sees Mrs Lowe, Mrs Cook and Mrs Istead. Mrs Istead is standing by a bicycle with a flat tyre.

John says, 'Hello ladies, can I help you at all?' Kind John.

Mrs Cook says, 'Mrs Istead has persuaded the parish council to buy this bicycle for use by any of the village residents. We were giving it a test run and the tyre went flat. We have a puncture repair kit, but can't get the wheel undone as it is bolted on too tightly.'

See John undo the wheel. See how strong John is. John helps the ladies to repair the puncture. See John put the wheel back on and Mrs Cook pump up the tyre.

Mrs Cook says, 'Thank you John. I keep this

stirrup pump at my house if you ever need one for your scooter. Would you like to test ride the bicycle John?'

'Yes please,' says John and gets on the bicycle.

See John ride the bicycle round and round the village green as fast as he can. When John is quite tired, he brings the bicycle back to the ladies.

'Thank you very much,' says John.

Mrs Lowe says, 'I like the way that you have plaited your beard so that it doesn't get in the way when you cycle. It looks very dashing. Perhaps you could let me ride on the handlebars like the lady in *Butch Cassidy and the Sundance Kid* did?'

John says, 'I don't think so, I might fall off and break a nail.'

Soon it is time for John to go home for lunch. See John scoot home as fast as he can. John is very hungry.

When John gets home, Janet is just stirring the sauce into the spaghetti.

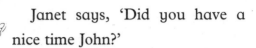

Janet says, 'Did you have a nice time John?'

'Yes,' says John. 'I stopped outside the village shop and saw Mrs Cook, Mrs Lowe and Mrs Istead. Mrs Cook offered me a go on the village bike. Mrs Istead, who soon had me mounted, was telling me she was being sponsored by the council to give something to everyone in the village. Mrs Lowe said that she liked my whiskers and wanted to know if she could have a handlebar ride and Mrs Cook said that she could let me have an old-fashioned handpump if I ever needed one.'

See Janet tip hot spaghetti down John's catsuit.

Hear the screams.

Poor John.

John Gets a Job with his Organ

Today, Janet and John are going shopping. John has some new shopping clothes – an orange silk brocade suit with a bright blue satin shirt, white platform boots and a green sparkly top hat. John is a popinjay.

As soon as Janet has strapped John into his safety seat they set off for town. Janet is a very good driver. John is not allowed to drive into town as he sometimes goes too fast. See the endorsements.

When they arrive at the shops Janet says, 'I have to go to the butcher's, the supermarket and the chemist's. I know that you sometimes get bored, so why don't you walk around to the park and play on the swings? I'll see you back here in an hour.'

Do you like swinging? John does.

See John wave goodbye to Janet as he hops and skips gaily down the road.

As John is skipping past the department store he sees Melanie Frontage. Melanie Frontage has a shop in the village that sells special things for people who are married. See the black windows.

'Hello Johnny,' says Melanie Frontage.

'Hello Melanie,' says John. What fun!

Melanie Frontage says, 'I'm just in town to help with a special promotion for the new department store. They have just opened and I am giving them a hand with the promotion. I'm just going to see the manager now. Would you like to come along?'

'Yes please,' says John.

When they arrive at the manager's office, she invites them in and says, 'Hello, my name is Mrs Weil, do come in. Are you part of the opening show?'

John says 'No, but I could play the organ for you.'

Mrs Weil says, 'We have hired a Hammond organ for the opening, it's just over by the perfume department. If you could play something between the dancers and the band that would be wonderful.'

John says, 'It's a few years since I played one of those.'

But soon he is playing very nicely. Clever John!

Do you think that 'Hammond organ' sounds like a cheap pie filling?

Mrs Weil says, 'Something classical and stirring would be quite good.'

John says, 'How about the *William Tell Overture*?'

Mrs Weil says, 'That would be perfect as it's nice and fast.'

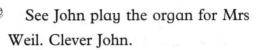

See John play the organ for Mrs Weil. Clever John.

Mrs Weil says, 'If you can come back tomorrow for the grand opening, I will pay you fifty pounds.'

John thinks of all the sweets and comics he could buy with fifty pounds.

Soon it is time for John to go back to meet Janet. See John skip merrily along the road. When John arrives at the shops he sees Janet.

Janet is pushing a big supermarket trolley full of shopping.

Janet says, 'Did you behave John?'

John says, 'Yes. I saw Melanie Frontage in town. She introduced me to Mrs Weil who was hoping for a little piece to spice up her opening. I was a bit hesitant at first, but I soon got my hand in. When we got down to it, she decided that she could squeeze my organ in between some of the other acts she had shown me, especially as I had a nice fast movement. I was tempted to milk it for

all it was worth but held back a bit as she said I could come back tomorrow and she would pay me fifty pounds.'

See Janet take all of the shopping out of the trolley and push John into the child seat. Do you know how all of the supermarket trolleys get into the river? John does.

Hear the gurgles.

Poor John.

John Goes to a
Posh Lunch

Today, John is going to a very posh lunch in a hotel in London. John has a part-time job reading out the names as people arrive.

The dinner is being hosted by a Scottish company, so John has to dress up specially.

See John put on a mauve tartan catsuit with a sparkly green bow tie, an orange fun-fur sporran and a lace ruff. John is a popinjay.

See John wave goodbye to Janet as he hops and skips down the road, his sporran flapping in the breeze.

When John arrives at the hall where the lunch is being held, he sees the lady whose husband is hosting the lunch.

'Hello John,' says Mrs Stephenson.

'Hello Mrs Stephenson,' says John. What fun!

Mrs Stephenson says, 'I'm sorry that my husband isn't here to greet you in person, but he is having a lot of trouble with his bow tie. I'm afraid he has already had a few drinks and he can't manage the knot. It's rather an old one, and probably a bit too tight. Can you help?'

'Yes,' says John. 'I know how to knot ties and cravats.' Clever John.

See John follow Mrs Stephenson back to her room and try to help her husband with his tie. While John is trying to get the tie knotted, Mrs Seagrave comes into the room.

Mrs Seagrave says, 'If it helps at all, I can let you borrow my husband's tie, he always has a spare with him.'

'Thank you Mrs Seagrave,' says John.

Mrs Seagrave says, 'As you are so good with this type of thing, perhaps you could help me with the pin on my lucky rabbit-foot brooch? It's quite old and the pin can be difficult to open.'

'Of course,' says John.

Soon John has fastened Mr Stephenson's tie and Mrs Seagrave's brooch and takes his place at the door ready to greet the guests.

Mrs Stephenson says, 'Thank you again John. Have you been to one of our lunches before?'

See John shake his head.

Mrs Stephenson says, 'Don't worry, it's very informal, but after lunch we like to sing our national song. Do you know "Flower of Scotland" John?'

John says, 'Is it McDougalls?'

Hear Mrs Stephenson laugh.

John says, 'I have been to Scotland. I even had my picture taken at Pitlochry.'

Soon the guests begin to arrive and John reads

their names from cards and
announces them. John is very
good at reading.

Soon everyone is seated and John is allowed to have some lunch too. See John gobble down his food. See the haggis stains.

After lunch Mrs Stephenson pays John some money and, as it is raining, puts him in a taxi to the railway station.

When John arrives home, Janet is doing the washing-up and making some toast.

Janet says, 'Did you have a nice time John?'

'Yes,' says John. 'It was a lovely lunch. When I arrived, Mrs Stephenson said that her husband had been drinking and was having trouble with his dickey, so asked if I would help out in her room. She told me that it was probably a bit too small and rather old. Then Mrs Seagrave got her Doug's out and asked if I could give her a hand with her lucky rabbit when I'd finished.'

See Janet sit John in the washing-up bowl and

hand him the toaster.

See John's beard go all frizzy.

Poor John.

John Goes on the Internet

Today, Janet and John are going into town. Janet is picking up some new net curtains and a new curtain rod for the hall.

As it is a lovely spring day, John puts on a bright yellow silk brocade coat with black trimmings, black trousers, a yellow frilly shirt and a black cap. John is a dandy.

Janet says, 'You look like an overripe banana.'

Can you stick out your bottom lip? John can.

When Janet and John get to town on the bus, Janet says, 'I'm going to the curtain shop. You can have a look around the town as long as you stay out of trouble.'

'I will,' says John.

See John wave goodbye to Janet and hop and skip gaily down the road.

John sees an Internet café. Are you allowed to use the Internet?

The lady who runs the café, Mrs Leach, says, 'Hello John. Are you shopping for clothes?'

'Not today,' says John. 'Most of the shops that I buy from are in London.'

Mrs Leach says, 'You could always look to see if they have a website.'

John says, 'I don't really know how to use the Internet.'

Mrs Leach says, 'Come on in, you will soon pick it up.'

See John sit down at one of the computers.

John sees Mrs Wiseman in the next seat. Mrs Wiseman is from Scotland. John has been to Scotland. John thinks that cleanliness is next to Inverness. Silly John.

Mrs Wiseman says, 'Hello John, I haven't seen you in here before.'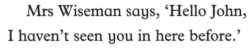

John says, 'No. I'm not allowed to use the Internet at home in case I break it.'

Mrs Wiseman says, 'I don't usually come in either, but my computer at home is broken, so I came in here to see if I could find a new table-tennis paddle on the Internet. My husband and I often play at home and none of the sports shops in town have any decent bats. Would you like to help me look?'

'Yes please,' says John.

Mrs Wiseman says, 'Do you use the mouse with your left hand or your right?'

John says, 'My right hand.'

Mrs Wiseman says, 'The Internet is a very good place to find things for people who are left-handed too. If you like, I'll show you what to do.'

See Mrs Wiseman show John how to use a search engine.

Mrs Wiseman says, 'This looks like the sort of

thing I want. They are replacement rubber facings for the bats. Can you read the technical description out for me please, as I don't have my reading glasses?'

'Of course,' says John.

John is good at reading. John used to read the news, but now the BBC just pays him to turn up once a week in his sparkly clothes.

Mrs Wiseman picks out some new rubber facings and pays for them with her credit card.

Mrs Wiseman says, 'Thank you John. You've been a great help. Now let me help you find what you are looking for.' Kind Mrs Wiseman.

See John and Mrs Wiseman look at all the shops that sell clothes for popinjays.

Soon it is time for John to go back to meet Janet. John waves goodbye to Mrs Leach and Mrs Wiseman and skips down the road to meet Janet.

John sees Janet coming down the road.

'Hello Janet,' says John.

Janet says, 'Did you behave?'

John says, 'Yes. Mrs Leach invited me into her Internet café. While I was there, Mrs Wiseman was telling me all about the indoor games she plays with her husband and said that she was looking for some new equipment. She said she was after a decent paddle, but hadn't had any luck, so she asked if I could help. She showed me some left-handed websites and instead of the paddle she decided she'd like to give some synthetic rubbers a try because they were guaranteed to increase the size of the sweet spot and improve length and ball placement.'

See Janet go purple.

Can you insert a curtain rod in a struggling newsreader?

Janet can.

Poor John.

Janet and John
Go for a Walk

Today, it is a lovely spring day and Janet and John decide to go for a walk by the river.

John puts on some sensible walking clothes – sparkly blue wellington boots, orange sequinned trousers and a bright pink angora wool jumper. John is a fop.

Janet says, 'Stop admiring yourself in the mirror or it will be lunchtime before we get started.'

John picks up his handbag and they set out down the lane.

When they get to the bridge by the river, Janet

sees Pastor Kidneys.

Pastor Kidneys says, 'Are you in a hurry Janet? I was just going to see Mrs Forrest but would like to talk to you about the spring fete if you have a few minutes? Mrs Forrest only lives around the corner.'

Janet says, 'Yes, of course.'

Janet says to John, 'I'm just going to see Mrs Forrest with Pastor Kidneys if you'd like to come along, otherwise you can play out here by the river as long as you don't get dirty.'

'I'd like to play by the river please,' says John.

Janet says, 'I shouldn't be too long. I'll see you back by the bridge at eleven o'clock.

Clever John can tell the time and has on his best Mickey Mouse watch.

See John wave goodbye to Janet and Pastor Kidneys and hop and skip down the path to the river.

When John gets to the river, he sees some people fishing.

John sees Mrs Roberts. Mrs Roberts is sitting on a stool and has two fishing rods.

'Hello Mrs Roberts,' says John.

'Hello John,' says Mrs Roberts. What fun!

John says, 'I didn't know that you liked fishing.'

Mrs Roberts says, 'Yes. It's a very relaxing hobby and it gets me out in the fresh air. Have you ever fished John?'

John says, 'Not since I was a young boy. I don't like the clothes people have to wear. You can't buy bright, sparkly fishing clothes.'

Mrs Roberts says, 'We wear green clothes so that the fish don't see us and get frightened. If you sit down here beside me, I'll show you what to do. Fishing is Britain's favourite outdoor pastime.'

See Mrs Roberts telling John all about her rods, reels and landing and keep nets. Mrs Roberts lets John hold one of the fishing rods. Mrs Roberts says, 'This is a carbon-fibre rod. My husband doesn't like them and prefers an old cane rod he has had for years.'

John says, 'Is the line supposed to twitch like this?'

Mrs Roberts says, 'Yes, you have a bite. What you need to do now is pull the rod back quite sharply.'

Mrs Roberts helps John to reel in the fish and picks it up with her landing net. Mrs Roberts says, 'This fish is called a chub. They are quite common in this river, but it's quite a small one so I think we'll put it back.'

Mrs Roberts helps John to bait his hook and soon John has another bite.

'You are getting good at this,' says Mrs Roberts and helps John to land the next fish.

John is very excited. See the damp patch.

Mrs Roberts says, 'This one is called a perch and it's quite a good size. We'll put this one in the keep net.'

Soon it is time for John to meet Janet. He thanks

Mrs Roberts and hops and skips gaily back to the bridge.

Soon Janet arrives. Janet says, 'Did you behave John?'

'Yes,' says John. 'I saw Mrs Roberts down by the river, she was telling me all about Britain's favourite outdoor pastime. She told me her husband doesn't like modern equipment and prefers the old-fashioned cane. After she showed me her fishnets, I was getting quite excited. I had a nibble and soon had a chub on. We finished off when she had a perch on my rod. She said I handled the tackle very well considering I was out of practice.'

Can you pick up a fully grown newsreader by the ankles and drop him in the river?

Janet can.

Poor John.

John Goes to the Insurance Broker

Today, John is going into town to get his clothes insured. Mr Boyd, who works with John, told him that his clothes are so bright that they might cause a fire in his beard. John is very worried. See the wrinkles.

John puts on a silver and orange sparkly catsuit with purple thigh-length PVC boots and a sparkly pink knitted hat covered in gold sequins. John is a popinjay.

Janet says, 'While you are out John, pick up a replacement stewpot for the one you got stuck on

your head last week.'

See Janet give John some money for the pot.

See John hop and skip merrily down the road, swinging his gold handbag.

John goes into the department store and buys a big cast-iron cooking pot, then scampers up the road to the insurance broker.

'Ding-a-ling' goes the office door.

'Hello John,' says Mr Spicer. 'What can I do for you today?'

John says, 'I'd like to insure my clothes in case they catch fire please.'

Mr Spicer says, 'Well, normally clothes are covered under a general household contents policy. Let me see what limit you have on your current insurance.'

See Mr Spicer looking up the details on his computer. Clever Mr Spicer.

John says, 'Can I put some numbers into the computer please?'

'Of course,' says Mr Spicer. 'The last time Janet called in, she increased the household contents cover to thirty thousand pounds with a five-thousand-pound limit on any one item. Are any of your clothes worth more than five thousand pounds?'

See John thinking very hard. John says, 'Probably not.'

Mr Spicer says, 'Well, you should be covered if there is an accident.'

'Thank you,' says John.

Just as John is about to leave, Mrs Udall-Waring comes into the office carrying a big bundle of dry-cleaning bags.

See John hold open the door and take the bags from Mrs Udall-Waring and hang the clothes up. Kind John.

'Hello Mrs Udall-Waring,' says Mr Spicer. 'What can I do for you today?'

Mrs Udall-Waring says, 'I'd like to insure my face as I am doing some modelling work for a magazine.'

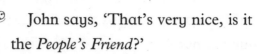

John says, 'That's very nice, is it the *People's Friend*?'

Mrs Udall-Waring says, 'No, it isn't!' See Mrs Udall-Waring do a cross face.

Mr Spicer says, 'That's quite a specialised form of insurance. We will have to go through a broker in London for that. Let me phone up someone and ask what is available.'

While Mr Spicer is on the phone, he tells John what numbers to type into the computer.

Soon Mr Spicer finishes talking to the man in London and says, 'Yes, we can provide you with some cover, how much did you want to insure your face for?'

Mrs Udall-Waring says, 'Twenty thousand pounds please.'

Mr Spicer taps some numbers into his computer and prints out a chart of prices. John takes the piece of paper off of the printer and gives it to Mrs Udall-Waring.

Mrs Udall-Waring is quite surprised by how

much it costs and says she will think about it.

John gives the clothes back to Mrs Udall-Waring and opens the door for her.

John is a gentleman.

John waves goodbye to Mr Spicer and skips all the way home.

When John gets home, Janet is in the kitchen.

Janet says, 'Did you remember to get the pot?'

'Yes,' says John.

John says, 'After I got the pot, I went to see Mr Spicer. When I was talking to him Mrs Udall-Waring came in. While I was hanging up her clothes, Mr Spicer was looking up her particulars. She said she wanted to get her face comprehensively covered, so I helped Mr Spicer with the entry on the table. I think it was probably a bit more than she was expecting though as she looked quite surprised.'

Can you make a noise like Big Ben with a cast-iron cooking pot?

Janet can.

See the big red lumps on John's head.

Poor John.

Janet and John
Go to a Car Show

Today, John has been asked to dress up as a motorist of the 1920s for the vintage car parade.

Do you like dressing up? John does.

John puts on bright yellow plus fours, orange and blue paisley socks, a red shirt and green waistcoat.

John is a fop and a dandy.

When they arrive at the car show, there are lots of people there already.

Janet says, 'It's rather a cold day, so I think I will sit in the café. You can come and find me

when the parade is finished. Try to behave for a change.'

'I will,' says John.

See John hop and skip into the car show to meet Mrs Hillerby, who owns the car in which John will be riding.

'Hello Mrs Hillerby,' says John. 'When is the parade please?'

Mrs Hillerby says, 'It's in about twenty minutes John. There are some displays going on outside if you'd like to watch.'

John goes outside to the arena. There are lots of big shiny cars. John sees a lady dressed in racing overalls getting out of a yellow sports car. The lady has a badge on that says, 'Mrs Ware'.

'Hello Mrs Ware,' says John. 'My name is John. I like the colour of your car.'

Mrs Ware says, 'Thank you John. You can call me Lucinda. If you'd like to give me a hand for a few minutes while I adjust the suspension to race setting, you can ride with me while I practise my display.' Kind Mrs Ware.

John watches while Mrs Ware gets under the back of the car. Mrs Ware says, 'Do you know anything about the MacPherson strut?'

John says, 'I used to go to Scottish country dancing, but I don't know that one.' See Mrs Ware laugh.

Soon, Mrs Ware has finished working on the suspension and climbs into the car with John.

Mrs Ware says, 'We're going to warm the tyres up a bit and then do some tricks.'

See Mrs Ware spin the back wheels and turn the car around in very small circles. Clever Mrs Ware.

See John clap his hands. Mrs Ware says, 'That's called a doughnut, it's a speciality of mine. If you have time after the parade, I can show you how to do it yourself.'

'Thank you,' says John, and hops and skips back to the parade ring.

See John ride round and round the parade ring

in Mrs Hillerby's car.

When the parade is over, John trots into the café to meet Janet.

Janet says, 'Did you have a nice time?'

'Yes,' says John. 'I was a little early to go on Mrs Hillerby's lap, so I went outside and saw the racing cars. I was talking to a nice lady and she asked if I could test the springs in the back of her car. Lucinda Ware helped a lot. She just had time to show me a few tricks, but said if I want to go back she will be happy to teach me how to burn rubber with her special doughnut.'

See Janet borrow a Bullnose Morris starting handle.

See John run.

Run, John, run.

John Goes to Work

Today, John is going to work. John works part-time as a junior traffic-boy on the radio. Do you know what the basic minimum wage is?

John puts on his best work clothes – a blue satin catsuit with white knee-length boots. See Agnetha Fältskog.

When John arrives at work, there is a couple waiting to go into the studio. John says, 'Is there someone looking after you?'

The man says, 'We're Mr and Mrs Quinn from Dublin and we're here to do an interview about food and drink.'

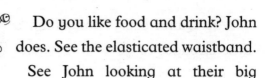

Do you like food and drink? John does. See the elasticated waistband.

See John looking at their big Tupperware boxes. Greedy John.

John says, 'What sort of food are you going to talk about?'

Mr Quinn says, 'It's mainly wholefoods. Mrs Quinn is very good with pulses.'

John says, 'Do you have any biscuits?' John likes biscuits.

Mrs Quinn says, 'Yes, I have some shortbread fingers.'

John says, 'Talking of Scottish short fingers, I'll just speak to the producer and let him know you're here.'

'Thank you,' says Mrs Quinn. 'Do you know if there are drinks available as I am a little nervous? I normally have a cup of coffee and a drop of Scotch if there is any.'

John says, 'There's BBC coffee.'

Do you know what BBC coffee tastes like?

Mrs Quinn says, 'Something a little stronger to go with it would be good.'

John remembers that his friend Lynn keeps a big bottle of Igor Tidy Welsh vodka under her desk and fetches a big glass for Mrs Quinn.

'Thank you,' says Mrs Quinn.

It is time for John to do his traffic report. See John wave goodbye to Mr and Mrs Quinn and go into his little cupboard.

Soon it is going home time. John puts his board games in his briefcase and catches the train home.

When John arrives, Janet is doing some ironing.

Janet says, 'Did you have a nice day at work John?'

'Yes,' says John. 'I met a very nice couple in the office. Mr Quinn said his wife was famous because she'd do anything with a pulse, but Mrs Quinn was a bit nervous. She said that she normally has a stiff Johnnie Walker chaser, but what I gave her was just as nice. But she did say that she preferred something a little harder.'

See Janet strap John to the ironing board and turn up the steam setting.

Hear the screams.

Poor John.

Janet and John Go to the Builders Merchant

Today, Janet and John are going to the builders merchant.

Janet has to get some solder and a new pipe bender.

Janet is good at plumbing. Clever Janet.

Janet says, 'Are you ready to leave yet?'

John is in front of the mirror adjusting the lapels of his leopard-skin boiler suit.

John is a dandy.

See Janet strap John into his safety seat and give him a barley sugar for the journey.

John likes barley sugar, but it makes his beard very sticky.

When they arrive at the builders merchant Janet wipes John's beard and says, 'They don't have a soft-play area John, so have a look around and try to behave.'

'I will,' says John.

See John walk around looking at all the shiny taps, pipes and toolbelts.

John has a toolbelt. It can hold his three hairdryers, seven nail files, four combs, a brush and has a big bag for all his make-up.

John is looking at the shiny gold shower fittings when he sees Mrs Holland.

'Hello Mrs Holland,' says John.

'Hello John,' says Mrs Holland. What fun!

Mrs Holland is from Yorkshire. See *Calendar Girls*.

Mrs Holland says, 'If you want one of these, you have to make sure that you have a large-bore pipe. We have one at home and we're going to need to fit a pump behind the bathroom cabinets. Come back and see me and I will give you a very good price.'

John says, 'I'd like a gold-plated shower too. I might ask Janet if we can have one.'

Mrs Holland says, 'They do show every mark, but they're ever so easy to fit. The trick is to make sure you've lined up the pipes with the mixer tap and greased them both before you fix them into the holes in the bath. Would you be doing the job yourself?'

'No,' says John. 'I have only just had a manicure, so I wouldn't want to spoil my nails.'

John thanks Mrs Holland and hops and skips back to see Janet.

Janet has just finished paying for the solder and the pipe bender.

Janet says, 'Who was that lady I saw you talking to?'

See the warning signs.

John says, 'That was Mrs Holland. I was looking at the pretty gold shower fittings. Mrs Holland said that because she only has a small-bore at home, she needed a pump behind the bathroom cabinets and she said she would give me a good price. She told me that if I was interested, the trick was to line up my riser and faucet between the apertures – and use plenty of grease.'

See Janet go purple.

Can you insert a newsreader into a pipe bender?

Janet can.

Hear the screams.

Poor John.

Janet and John
Go to the Park

Today, Janet and John are going to the park.

John likes going to the park and gets very excited. See the damp patch.

John changes into his best playing clothes – bright yellow dungarees with a blue satin shirt and silver wellingtons.

John is a popinjay.

Janet says, 'Don't forget to bring your dry-cleaning.'

'I won't,' says John. See John pick up the big parcel of clothes for the dry-cleaner.

When Janet and John arrive at the park, Janet sees Mrs Foden from the corner shop. Mrs Foden has a box of knitting needles for Janet.

Janet says, 'While I'm talking to Mrs Foden, why don't you take the dry-cleaning to the shop? You can buy an ice cream on the way if you like.'

'Yes please,' says John.

Do you like ice cream? John does. See the elasticated waistband.

See John hop and skip to Mr Hall's ice-cream van at the corner of the park. Mrs Crane is helping Mr Hall today as it is very busy.

'Hello John,' says Mrs Crane. 'What would you like today?'

John says, 'I'd like a maple and walnut ice cream please, with a walnut on top.'

Mrs Crane says, 'That's lucky, I only have one half-walnut left. That's a big parcel John, are you running away from home?'

'No,' says John. 'It's just some dry-cleaning.'

See Mrs Crane give John the ice cream.

See John rummage in his pocket for some money. John has to hold the ice cream with the same hand he is holding the parcel with. See John drop the ice cream. Hear John blub.

Mrs Crane says, 'There, there,' and dries John's tears. 'Don't worry John – look, the walnut didn't touch the ground so Bill will get you another ice cream and I will make you a sticky toffee banana milkshake for free while he's not looking.' Kind Mrs Crane.

When John gets back from the dry-cleaners, he sees Janet at the corner of the park.

Janet says, 'You were gone a long time, was there a queue at the cleaners?'

'No,' says John. 'I had a bit of trouble at the ice-cream van. Mrs Crane could see I was having difficulty keeping my package under control so she wasn't too surprised when I had an accident. While I was bent over, Mrs Crane managed to find my walnut, gave me a sticky banana shake under the counter and cleaned me up while Mr Hall wasn't looking.'

Can you nail someone's dungarees to a tree using knitting needles?

Janet can.

Poor John.

John Goes to the Jeweller's

Today, John is going into town to get his watch repaired.

Janet says, 'While you are in town, can you remember to pick up some bread? Do you want me to write a note for you so that you don't forget?'

'That's alright, I'll remember,' says John.

See John put on his orange leopard-skin coat and yellow floppy hat with a big feather.

John is a popinjay.

See John wave goodbye at the door and hop and skip gaily down the road.

When John arrives in town, he goes to the

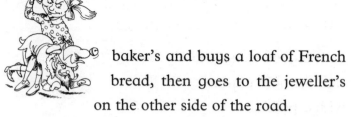

baker's and buys a loaf of French bread, then goes to the jeweller's on the other side of the road.

See John looking at the expensive Swiss watches in the window.

'Ding-a-ling' goes the shop bell.

'Hello John,' says Mrs Duncan.

'Hello Mrs Duncan,' says John. What fun!

Mrs Duncan says, 'How can I help you today John? Do you want to try on some more costume jewellery?'

'Not today,' says John. 'I need a new strap for my watch, the old one is broken.'

'Very good,' says Mrs Duncan. 'Let me show you what we have.'

See John looking at all the lovely watch straps.

Mrs Duncan says, 'Yours is quite nice for a dress watch, but I do like a nice big Rolex on a man. My husband likes digital watches. He and his friend were the first ones to buy the original Pulsar in the seventies. This one could really do

with a good clean and a service and the gold plating could do with a polish.'

John says, 'I know a trick to polish gold. Let me show you with your wedding ring.'

See John pull a piece of bread from the loaf and rub it on Mrs Duncan's wedding ring.

See the gold shine. Clever John.

Mrs Duncan says, 'All these years in the trade and I never knew that trick. Just for that, you can have a new watch strap for free.'

'Thank you,' says John.

John likes things for free. John is as tight as a BBC budget.

John thanks Mrs Duncan again and skips all the way home.

When John gets home, Janet is cooking some onion soup.

Janet says, 'Did you remember the bread John?'

'Yes,' says John. 'I saw Mrs Duncan too. I was admiring her Longines through the window. When

I went in, she said that her husband and his friend had a Pulsar together in 1971, just after they came out. She told me she prefers the larger Rolex on a man and said that it was about time I went back for a service. When I showed her how to polish her ring with a French stick, she gave me the strap for free.'

See Janet tip onion soup down John's trousers.

Hear the screams.

Poor John.

John Helps Out
in the Kitchen

Today, Janet and John are going Christmas shopping.

Do you like Christmas shopping? John does. John is very excited. See the carpet stains.

Janet says, 'Hurry up John! We don't want to be late for the bus.'

John has put on his special Christmas clothes – a red satin catsuit with white fur trimmings, a cape, patent-leather long boots and red sparkly glasses. See Elton John.

See Janet roll her eyes. Clever Janet.

When Janet and John get to the shops, Janet says, 'Why don't you have a look around the department store while I go and get some new tree lights from the market? I'll see you by the tree decorations display in an hour – and do try not to get into mischief!'

'I won't,' says John.

John runs up and down the escalators for a while and then hops and skips gaily to the toy department. John likes toys.

After John has played with all the toys, he goes to the cookware department.

In the cookware department, a lady is demonstrating how to cook Christmas dinner to a big crowd.

John likes Christmas dinner. See the redcurrant jelly.

Mrs Sutherland, the lady who is demonstrating, asks if anyone knows how to tell when a turkey is properly defrosted.

See John put his hand up and jump up and down.

Mrs Sutherland says, 'Yes, the spry old

gentleman with the beard. Do you know the answer?'

John says, 'Yes. You can tell when a turkey is properly defrosted when it has cobwebs in it.'

Silly John.

Mrs Sutherland asks if there are any volunteers who would like to help her prepare the meal. See John elbow grannies out of the way.

'Yes please,' says John.

John introduces himself to Mrs Sutherland and puts on a big chef's hat and an apron so that he doesn't spoil his clothes. Sensible John.

See Mrs Sutherland prepare the turkey for roasting.

Mrs Sutherland gives John a large chef's cleaver to cut up the vegetables.

Mrs Sutherland says, 'I'm trying out a couple of new recipes for stuffing this Christmas, so John will be making one and I will do the other one.'

See John chop vegetables and mix stuffing. See

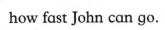

how fast John can go.

When the turkey is in the oven the audience gives John a big round of applause. See John blush.

Mrs Sutherland says, 'The turkey will be in the oven for some time now. The best way to tell when it's done is to turn it on to its back and wiggle the legs. If they move freely, it should be about ready.'

John says, 'I can't wait for the turkey to cook. Is there something I can eat now please?'

Mrs Sutherland says, 'Yes, I brought some sausage rolls along. They should be ready now.'

Can you eat a whole tray of sausage rolls? John can.

Mrs Sutherland laughs, 'Well, you must have been hungry John. Are you in charge of Christmas lunch at home?'

'No,' says John. 'Janet won't let me use sharp things in case of accidents.'

John says, 'Will you be cooking a turkey this

Christmas?'

'No,' says Mrs Sutherland, 'as there is just the two of us, a turkey is rather too big. We had guineafowl last year, and this year we have an organic goose.'

Soon it is time to meet Janet. See John wave goodbye to Mrs Sutherland and skip downstairs to the Christmas tree decoration display.

Soon Janet arrives. Janet says, 'Have you been a good boy?'

'Yes,' says John. 'I saw Mrs Sutherland. She was looking for someone to help her out with a big chopper, so I volunteered. She told me that her husband prefers smaller birds. She said she might get a goose if she's lucky and she was looking for a really good stuffing. She said you can always tell when a bird is finished, by turning over on to the back and wiggling the legs.'

See Janet pick John up by the baubles.

Hear the screams.

Poor John.

John Does the Housework

Today, John has to do some housework as Janet says she is 'nothing but a slave and is sick and tired of the mess'.

Janet says, 'I'm going to the fishmonger's. By the time I come back I want all that washing on the line and I want you working on that cockle-shell path around the pond. That sand and cement has been there since Christmas.'

John says, 'But I have a stiff neck from window-shopping on Saturday.'

Can you do a cross face? Janet can.

John puts on some old clothes – a Victorian

purple silk smoking jacket and fez, black trousers with a silver stripe and a white frilly shirt. John is a fop.

When Janet has gone, John empties the washing machine and takes the clothes out to hang them on the line. John does not know that you can take down the clothes prop, so he has to stretch. Silly John.

John is just pegging out his best lilac silk pyjamas when he sees Mrs Edwards from the insurance broker's. Mrs Edwards is from Essex. See the highlights.

'Hello Mrs Edwards,' says John.

'Hello John,' says Mrs Edwards. What fun!

Mrs Edwards says, 'I can see that you have a sore neck, can I give you a hand?'

'Yes please,' says John.

Soon Mrs Edwards and John have hung out all of the washing on the line.

John says, 'Thank you Mrs Edwards. I thought

I would have to take some junior aspirin before I could start work on the path around the pond, but it feels much better now. I even have time to go on the swing. Will you give me a push?'

See Mrs Edwards push John on the swing.

Mrs Edwards says, 'If you sit sideways on the seat, you can pretend you are on a horse. I used to do that when I played with the other boys and girls.'

See John smile.

Soon Mrs Edwards has to go. See John wave goodbye.

When Janet comes back, John is hard at work on the path.

'Hello John,' says Janet. 'I didn't think you'd have even started the path.'

John says, 'Mrs Edwards saw me in the garden hanging out my pyjamas and could see I was a bit stiff and trying to shake it off, so she gave me a hand. I told her that I thought I'd need a couple of

pills before the old cockle-work, but thanks to her I managed a quick swing. Mrs Edwards said that when she played with the other boys and girls she used to swing both ways.'

Can you hit a running newsreader with a frozen mackerel? Janet can.

Run, John, run.

Janet and John
Are Decorating

Today, Janet and John are decorating their house. Janet likes changing things in the house. Janet has just had new windows put in. See the chilblains.

Janet wants some new wallpaper, tiles for the kitchen floor, a new carpet for the bathroom and paint for the ceiling.

Janet says, 'Hurry up John, it's time to get ready to go to the DIY shop – and don't try accidentally leaving your wallet behind either.'

Do you know what a hairy old skinflint is?

John puts on some aquamarine overalls with

sparkly lilac trim, a green cap
and purple wellingtons.

John is a popinjay and a dandy.

Once Janet has strapped John into the booster
seat, they are ready to drive to the DIY store. John
plays with the toy steering wheel in the back of the
car and shouts at the other drivers.

Soon they arrive at the shop. Janet lets John
push the trolley along. What fun!

Janet says, 'Why don't you go and look for
some white paint for the ceiling? Even you can't
get that wrong!'

See John run with the trolley and make train
noises.

When John gets to the right shelf for ceiling
paint, he sees Mrs Coleman. Mrs Coleman is from
Scotland. See Jimmy Krankie.

Mrs Coleman says, 'I'm sorry John, my wee
cart is blocking the aisle.'

John says, 'Don't worry, I think I can get
through if you lean backwards a bit.'

See John carefully push his trolley past Mrs Coleman.

Mrs Coleman says, 'Do you know where I can find something to remove old gloss paint?'

John says, 'I use a blowtorch.'

Mrs Coleman says, 'Oh no, I wouldn't be any good at that, I can't stand all that smoke.'

John says, 'Well, you could buy some solvent that you paint on that is less messy. I'm sure you would be fine with that. Try aisle seven.'

Kind John.

'Thank you,' says Mrs Coleman.

John carefully reads the labels and picks up two tins of ceiling paint and takes them back to Janet.

Janet is buying some wallpaper, brushes and ready-mixed paste.

Janet says, 'You were gone a long time.'

John says, 'I saw Mrs Coleman, she said she was going to be doing some stripping and asked if I had five minutes. She said I had to be careful when I squeezed in because she had a "wee cart", so I told her to lean backwards and I'd try to miss it.'

See Janet fetch a ladder and paste John halfway up the wall of the DIY shop.

Poor John.

Janet and John Go to a Cricket Match

Today, Janet and John are going to a cricket match on the village green.

Do you like cricket? John does.

See John put on embroidered silk cricket whites with a mother-of-pearl sequinned cap and patent-leather cricket boots. John is a dandy.

John says, 'Can I take my space hopper please?'

Janet says, 'No,' and pulls John's reins.

When they arrive at the village green there are lots of people watching the cricket.

Janet says, 'I'm going to help Pastor Kidneys

with the tea. Can I trust you to behave?'

'Yes,' says John.

Janet says, 'I'll meet you by the beer tent at two o'clock.'

Can you tell the time? John can. Clever John.

See John hop and skip around the edge of the village green.

John sees some people playing on the practice pitch behind the church.

'Hello John,' says Mrs Dempsey. 'Are you any good at bowling?'

'Yes,' says John, 'but I can't field as I might chip my nail varnish.'

Mrs Dempsey says, 'That's alright John. Mrs Brown and I play for the ladies' team. We were just doing some batting practice in the nets and we need someone who can bowl to help us out.'

John says, 'Yes, I'd be happy to help.' Kind John.

See John rub the ball on his trousers until it is

nice and shiny.

John can only manage a short run-up because of the old trouble. See John bowling to the ladies. Clever John.

When John is quite tired he has to stop for a breather.

Mrs Dempsey says, 'Thank you John. I didn't know you could bowl leg-spinners quite so well.'

Mrs Brown says, 'Yes, that yorker had me in trouble too, though I did manage to hit that bouncer you delivered with the middle of the bat rather well, even if I say so myself. I normally duck those! You managed a couple of overs where we couldn't hit the ball at all.'

See John blush.

Soon it is time for John to meet Janet.

See John wave goodbye to the ladies and hop and skip gaily to the refreshment tent.

When John arrives, Janet is waiting.

Janet says, 'Where have you been? You're late.'

John says, 'I saw Mrs Dempsey and Mrs Brown

behind the church. They wanted someone to play with who could manage to deliver a good length, so I volunteered. Mrs Dempsey handled my googlies very well, while Mrs Brown managed to stroke a full toss right in the middle of the face without flinching. I told them that I could only manage two maidens before I got tired.'

Can you peg someone's beard to the ground with cricket stumps? Janet can.

See Janet fetch the motorised roller. Hear the screams.

Poor John.

Janet and John Go to the Village Fete

Today, Janet and John are going to a fete at the vicarage.

Do you know what a fete is?

Janet is going to help out on the refreshments stall and John is going to be a good boy and not put worms in his pockets like the last time. See John put on a pink silk morning coat with lime-green piping on the pockets and lapels, a green brocade waistcoat with gold buttons, silver and black striped trousers and gold shoes.

John is a popinjay.

See Janet wait for John to finish putting on his make-up. Kind Janet.

When they arrive at the vicarage, there are lots of people looking at the stalls.

Janet sees Pastor Kidneys. 'Hello Janet,' says Pastor Kidneys. 'Do you mind starting a little early as there are quite a lot of people here already?'

Janet says, 'Not at all.'

See Janet undo John's reins and wipe his face with the corner of her handkerchief. See John wriggle. Janet says, 'My elbow is still stiff from ju-jitsu on Wednesday. I don't want to have to put you across my knee again, so see if you can behave.'

'I will,' says John.

See John walk around all of the stalls. John stops at a stall selling old comics.

'Hello John,' says Mrs Marshall.

'Hello Mrs Marshall,' says John. What fun!

Mrs Marshall says, 'I am really busy this

morning. If you don't have something else to do, could you give me a hand please?'

'Of course,' says John. Kind John.

Mrs Marshall says, 'There are lots of old comics in bundles at the back of the stall, perhaps you could put them out on display for me?'

'Of course,' says John.

When John has finished putting all of the comics out, he helps to serve people.

John sees Mrs Davies.

'Hello John,' says Mrs Davies. 'I haven't seen some of these titles for years. Do you mind if I have a browse?'

'Not at all,' says John.

Mrs Davies says, 'I was really looking for some fake pearls for my niece's school prom, but now that I've seen these comics, I can see that I really must have some.'

See John take the comics from Mrs Davies and count them all up then work out how much to

charge. Clever John.

Mrs Davies says, 'Do you have a bag at all? I didn't remember to bring one with me.'

'Yes,' says John and helps Mrs Davies put the big bundle of comics and annuals in the bag. John says, 'I'm not sure all of these comics will go in one bag.'

Mrs Davies says, 'Pop it on the chair and I'll lean on it so you can get those last few in.'

See John push the last of the comics into the bag while Mrs Davies sits on it to make room.

John says, 'I think the cover on the *Twinkle* annual is a little bent and the cover from *The Whizzer* has come loose. Do you mind?'

'Not at all,' says Mrs Davies. 'I wanted them to read, not to collect.'

Soon most of the comics have been sold. Mrs Marshall gives John some of the last comics and some sweets for helping her out and John hops and skips off to find Janet.

John sees Janet on the refreshments stall.

Janet is doing the washing-up.

Janet says, 'Did you manage to behave?'

'Yes,' says John. 'I was giving Mrs Marshall a hand round the back and I saw Mrs Davies waiting. Mrs Davies said she was really after a pearl necklace but said that as soon as she saw my stand she knew I'd have what she was looking for.

'She wasn't sure that she could fit everything in and bounced up and down on my bag so hard that she nearly pulled the cover off of the old *Whizzer* and I ended up with a bent *Twinkle*.'

Do you know how to test whether your washing-up hands are as soft as someone's face?

Janet does.

See Janet hold John by the neck and push his head into the washing-up bowl.

See the bubbles.

Poor John.

John Goes Clothes Shopping

Today, John is going clothes shopping. Shopping for clothes is John's favourite thing, apart from redcurrant jelly.

John puts on his best shopping clothes – a pink sparkly morning suit with a pale green frilly shirt and a matching floppy hat with peacock feathers. John is a popinjay.

Janet says, 'Make sure you put your keys safely in your handbag John. I am going to pick up a belt sander from the hire shop to redo the parquet floor in the hall.'

See John wave goodbye to Janet as he skips

down the road to the bus stop.

When John arrives in town, he goes to the bank to get out his savings, then starts looking in all of the shop windows. John is very excited.

John sees a pretty aquamarine silk scarf with blue sequins and goes into the shop.

'Ding-a-ling' goes the shop bell.

John sees Mrs Bradley.

'Hello Mrs Bradley,' says John. 'How much is that pretty scarf in the window please?'

Mrs Bradley says, 'That scarf is on special offer at the moment. It is usually thirty pounds, but I could let you have it for fifteen.'

Do you like a bargain? John does. See John get out his purse and pay for the scarf.

'Thank you Mrs Bradley,' says John.

John puts the scarf in his handbag and goes outside. John sees a beautiful orange top hat in the window opposite. As John is about to cross the road, he catches the bottom of his yellow platform

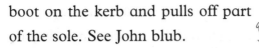

boot on the kerb and pulls off part of the sole. See John blub.

After John has dried his tears, he sees a shoe-repair shop and hobbles over the road.

John sees Mrs Ferris. Mrs Ferris is from Wales. See the consonants.

'Hello John,' says Mrs Ferris. 'I see you've had an accident.'

'Yes,' says John, 'but it's nearly dry now, and I damaged my boot as well.'

Mrs Ferris says, 'Take off your boot and let me see what I can do with it.'

John takes off his boot and hands it to Mrs Ferris.

John says, 'Will the repair take long, as I want to buy a hat, some white gloves and a new handbag and the shops close in four hours.'

Mrs Ferris says, 'No, the repair looks pretty straightforward. Would you like to help?'

'Yes please,' says John.

See John put on a leather apron to protect his clothes.

Mrs Ferris shows John the tools she will be using for the repair.

John says, 'What's this funny-looking machine for?'

Mrs Ferris says, 'That's a shoe stretcher. You can see that we can put in special inserts to help to relieve pressure on tender areas.'

John says, 'These boots do pinch a bit on my big toes.'

Mrs Ferris says, 'Well, let's see what we can do about that too. You should use a shoehorn though as the heels are starting to lose shape.'

See Mrs Ferris show John how to use the stretcher, then lets him use a stitching awl and then the last.

Mrs Ferris says, 'You are very good at this John. The adhesive on the new rubber sole is quite sticky now, would you like to apply it and trim the edges?'

'Yes please,' says John.

Soon John's shoe is as good as new and John

can carry on shopping.

When John gets home, Janet has already started work on the hall floor.

Janet says, 'You'd better come in the back door as I don't want you treading dust through the house. Did you get what you wanted?'

'Yes,' says John. 'As soon as I got into town, I saw Mrs Bradley. She made me a special offer and let me have exactly what I wanted at half the usual price. I was so excited that I had a bit of an accident. Mrs Ferris saw what happened and took me into her shop. She told me I would need to use the horn properly or I might start to lose stiffness in the back. She let me have her awl and stretcher, then showed me how she handled the cobbler's last.'

See Janet start the belt sander.

Can you hit twenty miles an hour in under three seconds?

John can.

Run, John, run.

John Plays Shopkeeper

Today, Janet and John are going to the supermarket.

While Janet is writing down a long list of things to buy, John is putting on his shopping clothes – a blue and white velvet sailor suit with matching hat, belt and handbag. John is a dandy.

When they arrive at the supermarket it is very busy and there is no room in the soft-play area, so Janet says, 'Why don't you walk around the shops instead of getting under my feet? I'll see you outside in an hour. If you manage to stay out of trouble, you can have a hot dog.'

John likes hot dogs.

See John wave goodbye to Janet and hop and skip along the road.

See John looking at his reflection in the shop windows.

John stops outside an antique shop with a big mirror in the window. John likes big mirrors.

See John go into the shop to look in some more mirrors.

'Ding-a-ling' goes the shop bell.

'Hello John,' says Mrs Oxborough. 'I didn't know you were interested in antique furniture.'

John says, 'I'm not normally, but you do have some lovely mirrors.'

Mrs Oxborough says, 'Would you look after the shop for me for a few minutes while I go to the bank?'

'Of course,' says John.

See John standing behind the counter playing at being a shopkeeper. A shopkeeper is a proper job. John does not have a proper job.

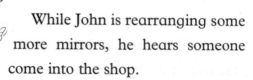

While John is rearranging some more mirrors, he hears someone come into the shop.

'Eh-up Fluffywhiskers,' says Mrs Bickerdyke. Mrs Bickerdyke is from Yorkshire. See Michael Parkinson.

Mrs Bickerdyke says, 'I didn't know you worked in here. Perhaps you can help me. I like a nice game of cards of an evening with my husband and a few friends, but my card table is looking a bit the worse for wear. I was really looking to either get a new one, or at least get someone to refinish the top of my old one. You don't seem to have any card tables here, so perhaps you can ask Mrs Oxborough whether she can get a new baize top fitted to mine? Or maybe you could do it? I could get my husband to take some before and after pictures for the parish magazine.'

Do you know how to get a word in edgeways? John doesn't.

John says, 'What sort of card

games do you normally play?'

Mrs Bickerdyke says, 'Generally we like a nice game of poker. My husband prefers Texas hold 'em, but I like five-card stud. We don't play for money though, but if you fancy it, I can sort you out with a good partner. That's very important, especially if you don't have good cards.'

John says, 'Thank you. I will ask Mrs Oxborough about the table when she comes back.'

Soon Mrs Oxborough comes back from the bank and John trots back to the supermarket to meet Janet.

'Hello Janet,' says John.

Janet says, 'Have you been a good boy John?'

'Yes,' says John. 'I was doing Mrs Oxborough a quick favour behind the counter in her shop when I saw Mrs Bickerdyke. She was telling me all about a game that she and her husband play with some of their friends. She told me that a decent partner was always much better than a good hand. Her husband likes a game called hold 'em, while she enjoys stud. She was telling me that I could play too. She also said that she wouldn't mind paying someone who could get felt and finish on her top with her husband taking pictures. Can I have a hot dog now please?'

See Janet pull John by his ear to the hot-dog stand.

See Janet tip hot fried onions down John's trousers.

Hear the screams.

Poor John.

John Goes for a Haircut

Today, John is going for a haircut. John goes for a haircut, beard-trim, tint and curl every week.

See John put on blue leather trousers, a leopard-skin shirt, a big blue floppy hat and a knee-length floral-print coat. Do you know what a popinjay is?

Janet walks with John to the hairdresser's. It is very cold today and John could not find any gloves to match his coat so he has very cold hands. Poor John.

When they arrive at the hairdresser's Janet says, 'I am going to pick up a Christmas pudding and some brandy. I'll meet you back here in an

hour. Try to behave this time!'
See Janet make a cross face. Janet
is good at cross faces.

John goes into the hairdresser's, takes his usual seat and rubs his hands together to try to get warm.

Donatella Noboddi says hello to John. Donatella is from Italy. See the frantic arm gestures.

Donatella asks John if he would like a cup of coffee. 'Yes please,' says John. 'Six sugars please.'

Donatella says, 'If your hands are cold, put them behind my laundry bins by the radiator, they will soon warm up.' Kind Donatella.

John drinks his coffee and gobbles down four biscuits. Greedy John.

Soon it is time for John's haircut.

Donatella says, 'Your hair has grown a lot since last time.'

'Yes,' says John. 'I give it two hundred brush strokes before bed every night to keep it nice and straight.'

Donatella says, 'It is very nice but you only need thirty or forty, two hundred is too many. You should use straighteners.' See Donatella use the electric straighteners on John's hair.

Then Donatella trims John's beard. John says, 'Should I use a special conditioner?'

Donatella says, 'No, it will be fine if I take off the ends where it is splitting. It is a lovely beard. Very manly.'

See John blush.

Soon Donatella has trimmed, brushed and tinted John's hair.

John admires his reflection in the mirror. See Liberace.

John pays for his haircut and gives Donatella an extra five-pound tip.

'Thank you,' says Donatella. 'See you next time.'

Janet arrives just as John leaves the hairdresser's.

'Hello Janet,' says John.

Janet says, 'They did a good job. You look like

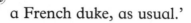

a French duke, as usual.'

'Thank you,' says John. 'As soon as I arrived, Donatella said I could warm up by putting my hands down the back of her trolleys. Then she sat me in the chair and said that it had grown a lot since I last saw her. She said I was probably stressing it by pulling at the root, so she showed me how to straighten it so I'd be able to keep it like that with only thirty or forty strokes.

'Donatella liked my manly growth and said it would be very nice once we'd got the end away, so I gave her an extra big tip.'

See Janet take out the Christmas pudding and rub it into John's hair.

John says, 'Why are you pouring brandy on my head and what are you doing with those matches?'

See John run.

Run, John, run.

John Gets a Part-time Job

Today, John is going to apply for a part-time job.

John spends all his money on fine silks, satin and lace. This makes Janet very cross.

Can you do a cross face? Janet can.

Janet says, 'If you think the money you earn as a part-time weather-boy makes ends meet, you are very much mistaken. You'd better go out and get another job or there will be no more new clothes for you. There are lots of jobs advertised in the London papers, if you don't have one by the end of this week there will be trouble.'

See John's lip tremble.

The next day, John has an interview in London.

John puts on his best interview clothes – a black velvet jacket with a diamanté picture of Lord Reith on the back, pink satin trousers, a frilly white shirt and a pink cowboy hat. See Elton John.

John waves goodbye to Janet as he hops and skips gaily down the road, making sure he touches all the lamp posts on the way for good luck.

Soon John arrives at the train station and catches the train into London.

Do you know where London is? John does. Clever John.

The job John has applied for is working for a magazine. John knows all about the news, but John is not a journalist and does not have a big red nose.

John rings the bell at the address he has been given. The door is opened and John introduces himself to the lady on the reception desk.

'Who are you here to see please?' says the receptionist. See John empty his pockets and look for the piece of paper with the name on it. See the sweet wrappers, comics, conkers, string and catapult.

John unfolds the piece of paper and says, 'I'm here to see Mrs Henderson.'

Soon Mrs Henderson comes down to meet John in reception.

'Hello John,' says Mrs Henderson.

'Hello Mrs Henderson,' says John. What fun!

Mrs Henderson says, 'We're looking for someone who knows all about what's happening in the news to work part-time on the breaking-news desk. I also need someone to stick up for me when the editor comes in,' laughs Mrs Henderson.

John says, 'I know all about the news. I work part-time at the BBC you know. I could be your right-hand man and let you have all of the insider stories.'

Mrs Henderson says, 'It's only for two days a week, and I think you might be just the right person. Is twenty pounds an hour alright?'

John thinks about all the nice clothes he could buy and says, 'Yes thank you!'

Soon it is time for John to go home. John catches the train back to Uckfield and buys some chips and a can of fizzy drink to have on the way home. See the sauce stains.

When John gets home, Janet is unblocking the sink.

'How did your interview go John?' says Janet.

John says, 'I was nice and early for the interview and got on with Mrs Henderson very well. She said I might have to stick up for her. I told her, I could be your star performer and insider view on the breaking-news desk twice a week.'

See Janet stick the sink plunger to John's forehead.

Can you swing a whole newsreader around your head?

Janet can.

Poor John.

Janet and John Go to the Vicarage

Today, Janet and John are going to the spring fair at the vicarage.

John is very excited. See Janet pack three extra pairs of pull-ups.

See John dress up in a green silk brocade frock coat, a frilly white shirt with lace cuffs and a bicorn hat with an ostrich feather.

John is a dandy.

When they arrive, Janet says, 'I'm going to help with the tombola. Why don't you go off and play some games? But no getting into trouble now!' See

Janet wag her finger.

See John hop and skip over to the playing field behind the vicarage.

There is jelly, ice cream, fizzy drink and cake. John likes cake. Do you know what bingo wings are?

There are also lots of games. Pastor Kidneys has a special prize game of hunt the slipper.

Do you like party games? John does.

Pastor Kidneys has hidden lots of old shoes around the vicarage grounds. Each one has a number on it and for each number there is a prize, with a special prize of ten pounds for the slipper with the number one on it.

Pastor Kidneys says, 'Cobbler, cobbler mend my shoe, get it done by half-past two' to start the game.

See everyone looking under bushes, in trees, behind hedges. John has caught some of the lace from the cuff of his shirt in one of Mrs Kidneys' thorn bushes and can't get it off.

See John blub.

John sees Mrs Ingram.

'There, there,' says Mrs Ingram. See Mrs Ingram get out her hanky, dry John's tears and help him free his sleeve from the thorn bush. See Mrs Ingram hand John the hanky so he can blow his nose. Kind Mrs Ingram.

John sniffs, 'But I haven't found any slippers at all yet.'

'Don't worry,' says Mrs Ingram, 'I'll help you look. I know where the first-prize slipper is as I saw Pastor Kidneys hiding it this morning.'

See Mrs Ingram show John where to find the slipper.

See John run all the way to Pastor Kidneys to claim the first prize. Lucky John.

See John skip over to the tombola to meet Janet.

Janet says, 'Have you been a good boy?'

'Yes,' says John. 'Mrs Ingram saw me with my hand in Mrs Kidneys' *Mahonia*. Once I'd had a great big blow I felt so much better. I told her that

I hadn't had any luck with the games, so she said that I might get lucky and get to slipper one behind the shed.'

Can you force a fully grown newsreader into a tombola? Janet can.

See John go round and round.

Poor John.

John Goes for a Check-up

Today, John is going to the doctor's surgery for a check-up.

John has to go to see the doctor to get his special pills as he is very old. See the bus pass.

Janet says, 'Don't be late John, you know that they are very strict about appointment times!'

See John putting on his tweed Dr Finlay suit with brown brogues, a white coat and a silver stethoscope.

Can you say 'stethoscope'? Terry can't.

Janet says, 'On the way back from the village, can you pick up some carrots for the roast this evening?'

'I will,' says John. John likes a roast. See the redcurrant jelly.

See John wave goodbye to Janet and hop and skip down the lane to the village.

When John arrives at the doctor's surgery he sees Mrs Jones.

'Hello Mrs Jones,' says John.

'Hello John,' says Mrs Jones. What fun!

Mrs Jones says that John's doctor, Dr Walmsley, is not in today, but Dr Sanderson will see him as she has a free appointment.

John sits in the waiting room and reads some old women's magazines.

John is halfway through an article about shelving when his name comes over the intercom: 'Mr Marsh to room seven please.'

When John opens the door, he sees Dr Sanderson.

'Hello Dr Sanderson,' says John.

Dr Sanderson says, 'Please call me Sue.'

'Is it just the usual prescription for your blue

pills today?' says Dr Sanderson.

See John blush.

John says, 'Yes please.'

Dr Sanderson says, 'Are you feeling quite well?'

John says, 'Yes, but I am a little worried about my weight.'

Dr Sanderson says, 'You don't look too overweight. You should try some of the local alternative medicine treatments. I'm usually booked up on a Friday as I have my herbal body toning treatment from the local practitioner, "The Whole Pharmacy". They have managed to tone up my thighs and bottom quite a lot. You should give them a try.

'While you are here, let's have a look at you.'

John says, 'Can I keep my Postman Pat socks on?'

Dr Sanderson says, 'There's no need to undress.'

See Dr Sanderson examine John.

Dr Sanderson says, 'I see you have your own stethoscope too. It looks the same as my husband Doug's.'

See Dr Sanderson show John the stethoscope

from the drawer in the surgery.

Dr Sanderson says, 'Consider-ing your age, you are very well. See you next month.'

See John pick up the prescription and hop and skip down the road to the chemist's, then to the greengrocer's to pick up the carrots.

When John arrives home, Janet is in the kitchen. 'Hello John,' says Janet. 'Did you get your pills?'

'Yes,' says John. 'I just had my nose stuck in an old *Woman's Realm* when Dr Sanderson called me. She normally has the men from The Whole Pharmacy firm up her bottom every Friday, but she managed to fit me in. She said that I'd got something that was very similar to her husband's and showed me her Doug's.'

See Janet go purple.

Do you know that carrots are good for your eyes?

See Janet select several large carrots.

See John's eyes water.

Poor John.

Janet and John Go to a Cider Festival

Today, Janet and John are going to a cider festival. Do you like cider?

John does, but he is only allowed one or two or he gets all grumpy and tired.

John puts on a sparkly blue catsuit with zebra-stripe detailing on the cuff and lapels, a big mauve floppy hat with a feather and black patent-leather boots. John is a fop.

Janet says, 'Hurry up John, for goodness' sake!'

John says, 'I just have to finish putting on my false eyelashes, but it's a bit fiddly.'

When John has finished looking at himself in the mirror for ten minutes, Janet pulls John's ear and takes him out to the car. Paint John's ear red.

Janet straps John into his booster seat, and soon they are at the cider festival. There are quite a lot of people there already. See the accordions. John is very excited. See the damp patch.

As soon as they are inside the marquee, Janet sees Pastor Kidneys. 'Hello Janet,' says Pastor Kidneys. 'I wanted to see you about the spring fair next month at the vicarage. Do you have time for a cup of tea and a chat?'

'Yes, of course,' says Janet.

Janet gives John his pocket money and says, 'You can have a look around. I'll see you back here in half an hour. Try to stay out of mischief.'

'I will,' says John.

See John looking at all of the stalls and displays. John sees Mrs O'Brien from the bank. Mrs O'Brien

 is from Essex. See the tattoos.

'Hello Mrs O'Brien,' says John.

'Hello John,' says Mrs O'Brien. What fun!

Mrs O'Brien says, 'It's quite a cold day today, I'm going to see Mrs Dickins on her stall. Her family has been making cider for centuries and they have some lovely hot mulled winter drinks that will warm us up. Would you like some?'

'Yes please,' says John.

See John hop and skip over to the stall, swinging his bright silver handbag.

John says, 'Hello Mrs Dickins.'

Mrs Dickins says, 'Hello John. Would you like a cup of our hot winter toddy?'

'Yes please,' says John.

See Mrs Dickins pour out two large cups and hand them over to Mrs O'Brien and John. See John nervously get out his purse. Mrs O'Brien says, 'Don't worry, I'll pay for these John.' See John look relieved.

Do you like spending money?
John doesn't.

John says, 'This is very nice,
what type of apples do you use?'

Mrs Dickins says, 'We get a lot of questions
about that. In Kent we don't use the same type of
sour apples that they use in the West Country, we
normally stick to sweet dessert apples such as the
locally grown orange pippin. We have just started
to produce a cider made from pears and one from
plums called "Jerkum". If you wanted to come
over to the factory, I'd be more than happy to
show you around and let you try some.'

Kind Mrs Dickins.

'Thank you,' says John.

See John have three more cups of cider.

Do you know how to walk on wobbly knees?
John does.

Soon it is time to meet Janet.

John waves goodbye to the ladies and weaves
unsteadily back to the café.

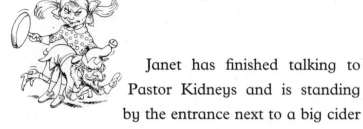

Janet has finished talking to Pastor Kidneys and is standing by the entrance next to a big cider press.

Janet says, 'There you are! Did you behave?'

'Yes,' says John. 'I saw Mrs O'Brien. She said that if I was free, she needed warming up and fancied some hot Dickins cider. The lady who was running the stall said that she'd had quite a lot this morning already and that she'd had a lot of interest in local cox, so if I wanted, I could go to her premises and sample her pear and Jerkum.'

Do you know how to fit a whole newsreader into a cider press?

Janet does.

Hear the screams.

Poor John.

Terry and Helen
Go to Slough

Today, Terry and Helen are going Christmas shopping in Slough. Do you know where Slough is? Terry does. Terry and Helen have a Slough postcode. See how proud Terry is.

Lady Helen says, 'Will you ever get a move on Ter'?'

Terry says, 'I can't find me dark glasses. I wouldn't want anyone to recognise me shopping in Slough.'

See Terry checking the pockets of his ermine robes.

Lady Helen says, 'If you don't hurry up, we won't get there before Primark closes and you need some new trousers. You keep wearing them out in the fork. We're supposed to be meeting Janet and John and I don't want us to be late.'

See Terry and Helen walk out to their car. Because Terry is very old, he has to have a nice man called Dennis to drive him to the shops. See Dennis help Terry into the car.

Soon, they arrive at the shops. Janet and John are already waiting in the car park. John has on an eighteenth-century French admiral's uniform with high boots and a feathery bicorn hat. John is a fop and a dandy.

Janet says, 'Ah, here they are now John. I'm going to the shops with Helen, I want you to take Terry to the library as neither of you can get into mischief in there. We'll meet you back here at four o'clock. Take an extra pair of pull-ups in your handbag in case you have an accident. Do try to behave!'

John says, 'I will.'

See John hop and skip gaily over to where Terry is being winched out of his car and into his buggy.

John says, 'Hello Terry.'

'That's Sir Terry to you, you gobdaw,' Terry says.

John says, 'Lady Helen said that we have to go to the library as they have a ramp for your buggy and it's nice and warm.'

Can you look all grumpy? Terry can.

Lady Helen says, 'Be sure to keep him away from the bookies. Since he went part-time on the radio, filling in before Elaine Paige, we've had to cut back a lot.'

See Lady Helen and Janet go off to the shops. See Sir Terry get his hip flask from Dennis. Thirsty Terry.

When John and Terry arrive at the library, see Terry wave people out of the way with his walking stick, and shout, 'Do you know who I am?'

See John wheel Terry through to the non-fiction section where all of the old people spend their afternoons. See the tartan blankets.

Terry says, 'I'm going on that computer over there.'

Terry knows how to use a computer. Clever Terry.

John sees Mrs Bickerdyke. Mrs Bickerdyke is from Yorkshire. See *Emmerdale*.

Mrs Bickerdyke says, 'Eh-up Fluffywhiskers! Have you come in to keep the old fellow out of the cold?'

See Terry throw his spare set of teeth at Mrs Bickerdyke.

John says, 'Janet and Helen have gone to the shops. I have just found a nice book about costume design from the late Elizabethan era. I don't see you in here very often.'

Mrs Bickerdyke says, 'I were always very interested in the showjumping on the telly in the

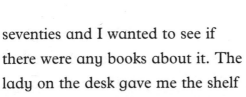

seventies and I wanted to see if there were any books about it. The lady on the desk gave me the shelf numbers, but it looks like all the books are right at the very top. Could you hold the library steps for me while I have a look?'

'Of course,' says John.

Mrs Bickerdyke says, 'My favourites were always Harvey Smith and Alvin Schockemöhle, but I can't find owt about them in these books. Perhaps Terry could look them up on t' computer?'

See Terry find lots of information about showjumping. Clever Terry!

Soon it is time for them to meet Janet and Helen.

When they arrive Janet and Helen are loading all of their bags into the car.

Janet says, 'Did you both behave?'

John says, 'Yes, we saw Mrs Bickerdyke. She was at the top of the ladder as she was after something sporting she used to enjoy in the seventies. She asked Terry if he wanted to look up Herr Schockemöhle while she was up there. I was just holding the ladder but had my mind on higher things.'

See Helen and Janet roll up their sleeves. See John run down the road pushing Terry's buggy.

Run, John, run.